William Hepworth Dixon

Free Russia

William Hepworth Dixon

Free Russia

ISBN/EAN: 9783742808158

Manufactured in Europe, USA, Canada, Australia, Japa

Cover: Foto ©Andreas Hilbeck / pixelio.de

Manufactured and distributed by brebook publishing software (www.brebook.com)

William Hepworth Dixon

Free Russia

COLLECTION
OF
BRITISH AUTHORS

TAUCHNITZ EDITION.

VOL. 1272.

FREE RUSSIA BY WILLIAM HEPWORTH DIXON.

IN TWO VOLUMES.
VOL. I.

TAUCHNITZ EDITION.

By the same Author,

PERSONAL HISTORY OF LORD BACON . . 1 vol.
THE HOLY LAND . . . . 2 vols.
NEW AMERICA . . . . 2 vols.
SPIRITUAL WIVES . . . . 2 vols.
HER MAJESTY'S TOWER . . . . 4 vols.

FREE RUSSIA.

BY

WILLIAM HEPWORTH DIXON.

COPYRIGHT EDITION.

IN TWO VOLUMES.
VOL. I.

LEIPZIG
BERNHARD TAUCHNITZ
1872.

PREFACE.

Svobodnaya Rossia—*Free* Russia—is a word on every lip in that great country; at once the Name and Hope of the new empire born of the Crimean war. In past times Russia was free, even as Germany and France were free. She fell before Asiatic hordes; and the Tartar system lasted, in spirit, if not in form, until the war; but since that conflict ended, the old Russia has been born again. This new country—hoping to be pacific, meaning to be Free—is what I have tried to paint.

My journeys, just completed, carried me from the Polar Sea to the Ural Mountains, from the mouth of the Vistula to the Straits of Yeni Kale, including visits to the four holy shrines of Solovetsk, Pechersk, St. George, and Troitsa. My object being to paint the Living People, I have much to say about pilgrims, monks, and parish priests; about village justice, and patriarchal life; about beggars, tramps, and sectaries; about Kozaks, Kalmuks, and

Kirghiz; about workmen's artels, burgher rights, and the division of land; about students' revolts and soldiers' grievances; in short, about the Human Forces which underlie and shape the external politics of our time.

Two journeys made in previous years have helped me to judge the reforms which are opening out the Japan-like empire of Nicolas into the Free Russia of the reigning prince.

February, 1870.
6 St. James' Terrace.

NOTE.

A few slips of the pen, and some errors of the press, which escaped my eye in the earlier proofs, have been removed from the text in this new edition.

April, 1870.

CONTENTS

OF VOLUME I.

		Page
CHAPTER I.	Up North	9
— II.	The Frozen Sea	17
— III.	The Dvina	24
— IV.	Archangel	31
— V.	Religious Life	39
— VI.	Pilgrims	47
— VII.	Father John	56
— VIII.	The Vladika	66
— IX.	A Pilgrim Boat	74
— X.	The Holy Isles	83
— XI.	The Local Saints	91
— XII.	A Monastic Household	100
— XIII.	A Pilgrim's Day	108
— XIV.	Prayer and Labour	117
— XV.	Black Clergy	126
— XVI.	Sacrifice	136
— XVII.	Miracles	145
— XVIII.	The Great Miracle	156
— XIX.	A Convent Spectre	168
— XX.	Story of a Grand Duke	173

CONTENTS OF VOLUME I.

		Page
CHAPTER XXI.	Dungeons	181
— XXII.	Nicolas Ilyin	190
— XXIII.	Adrian Pushkin	200
— XXIV.	Dissent	208
— XXV.	New Sects	219
— XXVI.	More New Sects	225
— XXVII.	The Popular Church	233
— XXVIII.	Old Believers	243
— XXIX.	A Family of Old Believers	248
— XXX.	Cemetery of the Transfiguration	257
— XXXI.	Ragoski	266
— XXXII.	Dissenting Politics	275
— XXXIII.	Conciliation	281

FREE RUSSIA.

CHAPTER I.

Up North.

"White Sea!" laughs the Danish skipper, curling his thin red lip; "it is the colour of English stout. The bed may be white; being bleached with the bones of wrecked and sunken men; but the waves are never white, except when they are ribbed into ice and furred with snow. A better name is that which the sailors and seal-fishers give it,—the Frozen Sea."

Rounding the North Cape, a weird and hoary mass of rock, projecting far into the Arctic foam, we drive in a south-east course, lashed by the wind, and beaten by hail and rain, for two long days, during which the sun never sets and never rises, and in which, if there is dawn at the hour of midnight, there is also dusk at the time of noon.

Leaving the picturesque lines of fiord and alp behind, we run along a dim, unbroken coast, not often to be seen through the pall of mist, until, at the end of some fifty hours, we feel, as it were, the land in our front; a stretch of low-lying shore in the vague and far-off distance, trending away towards the south, like the trail of an evening cloud. We bend in a southern course, between Holy Point (Sviatoi Noss, called on our charts, in rough salt slang, Sweet Nose), and Kanin Cape, towards the Corridor; a strait some thirty miles wide, leading down from the Polar ocean into that vast irregular dent in the northern shore of Great Russia known as the Frozen Sea.

The land now lying on our right, as we run through the Corridor, is that of the Lapps; a country of barren downs and deep black lakes; over which a few trappers and fishermen roam; subjects of the Tsar and followers of the Orthodox rite; but speaking a language of their own, not understood in the Winter Palace, and following a custom of their fathers, not yet recognised in St. Isaac's Church. Lapland is a tangle of rocks and pools; the rocks very big and broken, the pools very deep and black; with here and there a valley winding through them, on the slopes of which grows a little reindeer moss. Now and then you come upon a patch of birch and pine. No grain will grow in these Arctic zones, and the food of the natives is game and fish. Ryebread, their only luxury, must be fetched in boats from the towns of Onega and Archangel, standing on the shores of the Frozen Sea, and fed from the warmer provinces in the South. These Lapps are still nomadic; cowering through the winter months in shanties; sprawling through the summer months in tents. Their shanty is a log pyramid, thatched with moss to keep out wind and sleet; their tent is of the Comanche type; a roll of reindeer skins drawn slackly round a pole, and opened at the top to let out smoke.

A Lapp removes his dwelling from place to place, as the seasons come and go; now herding game on the hill-sides, now whipping the rivers and creeks for fish; in the warm months, roving inland in search of moss and grass; in the frozen months, drawing nearer to the shore in search of seal and cod. The men are equally expert with the bow, their ancient weapon of defence, and with the birding-piece, the arm of settlers in their midst. The women, looking anything but lovely in their seal-skin tights and reindeer smocks, are infamous for magic and second sight. In every district of the North, a female Lapp is feared as a witch—an enchantress—who keeps a devil at her side, bound by the powers of darkness to obey her will. She can see into the coming day. She can bring a man ill-luck. She can throw herself out into space, and work upon ships that are sailing past her on the sea. Far out in the Polar brine, in waters where her countrymen fish for cod, stands a lump of rock, which the crews regard as a Woman and her Child. Such fantasies are common in these Arctic seas, where the waves wash in and out through the cliffs, and rend and carve them into wondrous shapes. A rock on the North Cape is called the Friar; a group of islets near that cape is known as the Mother and her Daughters. Seen through the veil of Polar mist, a block of stone may take a mysterious form; and that lump of rock in the Polar waste, which the cod-fishers say is like a woman with her child, has long been known to them as the Golden Hag. She is rarely seen; for the clouds in summer, and the snows in winter, hide her charms from the fishermen's eyes; but when she deigns to show her face in the clear bright sun, her children hail her with a song of joy, for on seeing her face they know that their voyage will be blessed by a plentiful harvest of skins and fish.

Woe to the mariner tossed upon their coast!

The land on our left is the Kanin peninsula; part of that region of heath and sand over which the Samoyed roams; a desert of ice and snow, still wilder than the countries hunted by the Lapp. A land without a village, without a road, without a field, without a name; for the Russians who own it have no name for it save that of the Samoyeds' Land; this province of the great empire trends away north and east from the walls of Archangel and the waters of Kanin Cape to the summits of the Ural chain and the Iron Gates of the Kara Sea. In her clefts and ridges snow never melts; and her shore-lines, stretching towards the sunrise upwards of two thousand miles, are bound in icy chains for eight months in the twelve. In June, when the winter goes away, suddenly, the slopes of a few favoured valleys grow green with reindeer moss; slight specks of verdure in a landscape which is even then dark with rock and grey with rime. On this green moss the reindeer feed, and on these camels of the Polar zone the wild men of the country live.

Samoyed means cannibal—man-eater; but whether the men who roam over these sands and bogs deserve their evil fame is one of the questions open to new lights. They use no fire in cooking food; and perhaps it is because they eat the reindeer raw that they have come to be accused of fondness for human flesh. In chasing the game on which they feed, the Samoyeds crept over the Ural mountains from their far-off home in the north of Asia, running it down in a tract too cold and bare for any other race of men to dwell on. Here the Zarayny found them, thrashed them, set them to work.

These Zarayny, a clever and hardy people, seem connected in type and speech with the Finns; and they are thought to be the remnant of an ancient colony of trappers. Fairer than the Samoyeds, they live in log-huts like other Russians, and are rich in herds of reindeer, which they compel the Samoyeds to tend like slaves. This service to the higher race is slowly changing the savage Samoyed into a civilised man; since it gives him a sense of property and a respect for life. A red man kills the beast he hunts; kills it beyond his need, in the animal wantonness of strength. A Samoyed would do the same; but the Zarayny have taught him to rear and tend, as well as to hunt and snare, his food. A savage, only one degree above the Pawnee and the Ute, a Samoyed builds no shed; plants no field; and owns no property in the soil. He dwells, like the Lapp, in a tent; a roll of skins, sewn on to each other with gut, and twisted round a shaft, left open at the top, and furnished with skins to lie on like an Indian lodge. No art is lavished on this roll of skin; not so much as the totem which a Cheyenne daubs on his prairie tent. Yet the Samoyed has notions of village life, and even of government. A collection of tents he calls a Choom; his Choom is ruled by a medicine-man; the official name for whom in Russian society is a Pope.

The reigning Emperor has sent some priests to live among these tribes, just as in olden times Marfa of Novgorod sent her popes and monks into Lapland and Karelia; hoping to divert the natives from their Pagan habits and bring them over to the church of Christ. Some good, it may be hoped, is done by these Christian priests; but a Russ who knows the country and the people smiles when you ask him about their doings in the Gulf of Obi and around the Kara Sea. One of these missionaries whom I chanced to meet, had pretty well ceased to be a civilised man. In name, he was a pope; but he lived and dressed like a medicine-man; and he was growing into the likeness of a Mongol in look and gait. Folk said he had taken to his bosom a native witch.

Through the gateway held by these tribes we enter into Russia—Great Russia; that country of the old Russians, whose plains and forests the Tartar horsemen never swept.

Why enter Russia by these northern gates? If the Great Mogul had conquered England in the seventeenth century; if Asiatic manners had been paramount in London for two hundred years; if Britain had recovered her ancient freedom and civil life; where would a foreign observer, anxious to see the English as they are, begin his studies? Would he not begin them in Massachusetts rather than in Middlesex, even though he should have to complete his observations on the Mersey and the Thames?

A student of the Free Russia born of the Crimean War, must open his work of observation in the northern zones; since it is only within this region of lake and forest that he can find a Slavonic race which has never been tainted by foreign influence, never been broken by foreign yoke. The zone from Onega to Perm—a country seven times larger than France—was colonized from Novgorod the Great, while Novgorod was yet a Free City; rich in trade, in piety, in art; a rival of Frankfort and Florence; and, like London and Bruges, a station of the Hanseatic League. Her colonies kept the charter of their freedom safe. They never bent to the Tartar yoke, nor learned to walk in the German ways. They knew no masters, and they held no serfs. "We never had amongst us," said to me an Archangel farmer, "either a noble or a slave." They clung, for good and evil, to their ancient life; and when the Patriarch Nikon reformed the Church in a Byzantine sense (1667), as the Tsar Godounof had transformed the Village in a Tartar sense (1601), they disowned their Patriarch just as they had denied their Tsar. In spite of every force that could be brought against them by a line of autocrats, these free colonists have not been driven into accepting the reformed Official liturgies in preference to their Ancient rites. They kept their native speech, when it was ceasing to be spoken in the capital; and when the time was ripe, they sent out into the world a boy of genius, peasant-born and reared (the Poet, Michael Lomonosof), to impose that popular language on the college, on the senate, on the court.

CHAPTER II.

The Frozen Sea.

At Cape Intsi we pass from the narrow straits dividing the Lapp country from the Samoyed country into this northern gulf.

About twice the size of Lake Superior in the United States, this Frozen Sea has something of the shape of Como; one narrow northern bay, extending to the town of Kandalax, in Russian Lapland; and two southern bays, divided from each other by a broad sandy peninsula, the home of a few villagers employed in snaring cod and hunting seal. These southern bays are known, from the rivers which fall into them, as Onega Bay and Dvina Bay. At the mouths of these rivers stand the two trading ports of Onega and Archangel.

The open part of this inland gulf is deep—from sixty to eighty fathoms; and in one place off the entrance into Kandalax Bay, the line goes down no less than a hundred and sixty fathoms. Yet the shore is neither steep nor high. The gulf of Onega is rich in rocks and islets; many of them only banks of sand and mud, washed out into the sea from the uplands of Kargopol; but in the wide entrance of Onega Bay, between Orlof Point and the town of Kem, stands out a notable group of islets—Solovetsk, Anzersk, Moksalma, Zaet and others; islets which play a singular part in the history of Russia, and connect themselves with curious legends of the Imperial court.

In Solovetsk, the largest of this group of islets, stands the famous Convent of that name; the house of Saints Savatie and Zosima; the refuge of St. Philip; the shrine to which emperors and peasants go on pilgrimage; the haunt of that Convent Spectre which one hears described in the cod-fisher's boat and in the Kozak's tent; the scene of many great events, and of One event which Russians have agreed to sing and paint as the most splendid miracle of these latter days.

Off the Dvina bar stands the new tower and lighthouse, where the pilots live; a shaft some eighty feet high, not often to be seen above the hanging drapery of fog. A pilot comes on board; a man of soft and patient face, with grey-blue eyes, and flow of brownish hair, who tells us in a bated tone,—as though he feared we might be vexed with him and beat him,—that the tide is ebbing on the bar, and we shall have to wait for the flow. "Wait for the tide!" snaps our Danish jarl; "stand by, we'll make our course," The sun has just peeped out from behind his veil; but the clouds droop low and dark, and every one feels that a gale is coming on. Two barks near the bar,—the "Thera" and the "Olga,"—bob and reel like tipsy men; yet our pale Russ pilot, urged by the stronger will, gives way with a smile; and our speed being lowered by half, we push on slowly towards the line of red and black signals floating in our front.

The "Thera" and the "Olga" are soon behind us, shivering in all their sheets, like men in the clutch of ague,—left in our wake to a swift and terrible doom. In half an hour we pass the line of buoys, and gain the outer port.

Like all great rivers, the Dvina has thrown up a delta of isles and islets near her mouth, through which she pours her flood into the sea by a dozen arms. None of these dozen arms can now be laid down as her main entrance; for the river is more capricious than the sea; so that a skipper who leaves her by one outlet in August, may have to enter by another when he comes back to her in June. The main passage in the old charts flowed past the convent of St. Nicolas; then came the turn of Rose island; afterwards the course ran past the guns of Fort Dvina; but the storms which swept the Polar seas two summers since, destroyed that passage as an outlet for the larger kinds of craft. The port police looked on in silence. What were they to do? Archangel was cut off from the sea, until a Danish blacksmith, who had set up forge and hammer in the new port, proposed that the foreign traders should hire a steamer and find a deliverance for their ships. "If the water goes down," he said, "it must have made a way for itself. Let us try to find it out." A hundred pounds were lodged in the bank, a steamer was hired, and a channel, called the Maimax Arm, was found to be deep enough for ships to pass. The work was done, the city opened to the sea; but then came the question of port authorities and their rules. No bark had ever left the city by this Maimax Arm; no rules had been made for such a course of trade; and the port police could not permit a ship to sail unless her papers were drawn up in the usual forms. In vain the merchants told them the case was new, and must be governed by a rule to match. They might as well have reasoned with a Turkish bey. Here rode a fleet of vessels, laden with oats and deals for the Elbe, the Maas, and the Thames; there ran the abundant Maimax waters to the sea; but the printed rules of the port, unconscious of the freaks of nature and of the needs of man, forbade this fleet to sail.

Appeal was made to Prince Gagarine, governor of Archangel; but Gagarine, though he laughed at these port rulers and their forms, had no deals and grain of his own on board the ships. Gospodin Sredine, a keen-witted Master of the Customs, tried to open the ports and free the ships by offering to put officers on the new channel; but the police were— the police. In vain they heard that the goods might spoil, that the money they cost was idle, and that every ruble wasted would be so much loss to their town.

To my question, "How was it arranged at last?" a skipper, who was one of the prisoners in the port, replies, "I will tell you in a word. We sent to Petersburg; the minister spoke to the Emperor; and here is what we have heard they said. 'What's all this row in Archangel about?' asks the Emperor. 'It is all about a new mouth being found in the Dvina, Sir, and ships that want to sail down it, Sir, because the old channel is now shoaled up, Sir.'

'In God's name,' replies the Emperor, 'let the ships go out by any channel they can find.'"

Whether the thing was done in this sailor-like way, or by the more likely method of official report and order, the Maimax mouth was opened to the world in spite of the port-police and their printed rules.

A Hebrew of the olden time would have called this sea a whited sepulchre. Even men of science, to whom wintry storms may be summed up in a line of figures—so many ships in the pack, so many corpses on the beach—can find in the records of this frozen deep some show of an excuse for that old Lapland superstition of the Golden Hag. The year before last was a tragic time, and the memory of one dark day of wrack and death has not yet had time to fade away.

At the end of June, a message, flashed from the English Consul at Archangel—a man to represent his country on these shores,—alarmed our Board of Trade by such a cry for help as rarely reaches a public board. A hundred ships were perishing in the ice. These ships were Swedes, Danes, Dutch, and English; luggers, sloops, corvettes, and smacks; all built of wood, and many of them English manned. Could anything be done to help them? "Help is coming," flashed the wires from Charing Cross; and on the first day of July, two steamers left the Thames to assist in rescuing those ships and men from the Polar ice. On the fifteenth night from home these English boats were off Cape Gorodetsk on the Lapland coast, and when morning dawned they were striving to cross the shallow Archangel bar. They could not pass; yet the work of humanity was swiftly and safely done by the English crews.

That fleet of all nations, English, Swedish, Dutch, and Danish, left the Dvina ports on news coming up the delta that the pack was breaking up in the gulf; but on reaching that Corridor, through which we have just now come, they met the ice swaying to and fro, and crashing from point to point, as the changing wind veered round from north to south. By careful steering they went on, until they reached the straits between Kanin Cape and Holy Point. The ice in their front was now thick and high; no passage through it could be forced; and their vessels reeled and groaned under the blows which they suffered from the floating drifts. A brisk north wind arose, and blowing three days on without a pause, drove blocks and bergs of ice from the Polar ocean down into the gut, forcing the squadrons to fall back, and closing up every means of escape into the open sea. The ships rolled to and fro, the helmsmen trying to steer them in mid-channel, but the currents were now too strong to stem, and the helpless craft were driven upon the Lapland reefs, where the crews soon saw themselves folded and imprisoned in the pack of ice.

Like shots from a fort, the crews on board the stronger ships could hear in the grim waste around them hull after hull crashing up, in that fierce embrace, like fine glass trinkets in a strong man's hand. When a ship broke up and sank, the crew leaped out upon the ice and made for the nearest craft, from which in a few hours more they might have to fly in turn. One man was wrecked five times in a single day; each of the boats to which he clung for safety parting beneath his feet and gurgling down into the frozen deep.

When the tale of loss was made up by the relieving steamers, this account was sent home to the Board of Trade:

The number of ships abandoned by their crews was sixty-four; of this great fleet of ships, fourteen were saved and fifty lost. Of the fifty ships lost in those midsummer days, eighteen were English built and manned; and the master mentions with a noble pride, that only one ship flying the English flag was in a state to be recovered from the ice after being abandoned by her crew.

It would be well for our fame if the natives had no other tales to tell of an English squadron in the Frozen Sea.

CHAPTER III.

The Dvina.

By the Maimax arm we steam through the delta for some twenty miles; past low, green banks and isles like those in the Missouri bed; though the loam in the Dvina is not so rich and black as that on the American stream. Yet these small isles are bright with grass and scrub. Beyond them, on the mainland, lies a fringe of pines, going back into space as far as the eye can pierce.

The low island, lying on your right as you scrape the bar, is called St. Nicolas, after that sturdy priest, who is said to have smitten the heretic Arius on his cheek. No one knows where this Nicolas lived and died; for it is clear from the Acta that he had no part in the Council of Nice. The Book of Saints describes him as born in Liki and living in Mira; whence they call him the Saint of Mirliki; but not a line of his writing is extant, and the virtues assigned to him are of opposing kinds. He is a patron of nobles and of children, of sailors, of cadgers, and of pilgrims. Yet, in spite of his doubtful birth and genius, Nicolas is a popular saint. Poor people like him as one who is good to the poor; a friend of beggars, fishermen, and tramps. A Russian turns to him as the hope of starving and drowning men; so that his name is often heard, his image often seen, in these northern wilds; more than all else, on the banks of rivers and on the margins of the frozen sea. A peasant learns with delight from his Book of Saints (his Bible, Epos, Drama, Code, and History, all in one) that Nicolas is the most potent saint in heaven; sitting on the right hand of God; and having a cohort of three hundred angels, armed and ready to obey his nod. A mujik asked a foreign friend to tell him, who will be God when God dies? "My good fellow," said he, smiling, "God will never die." At first the peasant seemed perplexed. "Never die!" and then a light fell on him. "Yes," he retorted, slowly; "I see it now. You are an unbeliever; you have no religion. Look you; I have been better taught. God will one day die; for He is very old; and then St. Nicolas will get his place."

Though he is common to all Russians—adored on the Dnieper, on the Volkhof, on the Moskva, no less than on the Dvina—he is worshipped with peculiar zeal in these northern zones. Here he is the sailor's saint, the adventurer's help; and all the paintings of him show that his watchful eyes are bent in eager tenderness upon the swirl and passion of the Frozen Sea. This delta might be called his province; for not only was the island on your right called after him, but also the ancient channel, and the bay itself. The oldest cloister in the district bears his name.

On passing into the Maimax arm, your eyes— long dimmed by the sight of sombre rock, dark cloud, and sullen surf—are charmed by soft, green grass and scrub; but the sight goes vainly out, through reeds and copse, in search of some cheery note of house and farm. One log-hut you pass, and only one. Two men are standing near a bank, in a little clearing of the wood; a lad is idling in a frail canoe, which the wash of your steamer lifts and laves; but no one lodges in the shed; the men and boy have come from a village some miles away. Dropping down the river in their boat to cut down grass for their cows, and gather up fuel for their winter fires, they will jump into their canoe at vespers, and hie them home.

On the banks of older channels the villages are thick; slight groups of sheds and churches, with a cloister here and there, and a scatter of wind-mills whirling against the sky; each village and mill in its appointed place, without the freak and medley of original thought. Here nothing is done by individual force; a pope, an elder, an imperial officer, must have his say in every case; and not a mouse can stir in a Russian town, except by leave of some article in a printed code. Fort Dvina was erected on a certain neck of land in the ancient river-bed, and Nature was expected to conform herself for ever to the order fixed by imperial rule.

On all these banks you note a forest of memorial crosses. When a sailor meets with bad weather, he goes on shore and sets up a cross. At the foot of this symbol he kneels in prayer, and when a fair wind rises, he leaves his offering on the lonely coast. When the peril is sharp, the whole ship's crew will land, cut down and carve tall trees, and set up a memorial with names and dates. All round the margins of the frozen sea these pious witnesses abound; and they are most of all numerous on the rocks and banks of the Holy Isles. Each cross erected is the record of a storm.

Some of these memorial crosses are historic marks. One tree, set up by Peter the Great when he escaped from the wreck of his ship in the frozen deep, has been taken from the spot where he planted it, and placed in the cathedral at Archangel. "This cross was made by Captain Peter," says a tablet cut in the log by the Emperor's own knife; and Peter being a carver in wood and stone, the work is not without touches of art and grace. Might not a word be urged in favour of this custom of the sea which leaves a picture and a blessing on every shore? An English mariner is apt to quit a coast on which he has been kept a prisoner by adverse winds with a curse in his heart and a bad name on his tongue. Jack is a very grand fellow in his way; but surely there is a beauty, not less winning than the piety, in this habit of the Russian tar.

Climbing up the river, you come upon fleets of rafts and praams, on which you may observe some part of the native life. The rafts are floats of timber—pine-logs, lashed together with twigs of willow, capped with a tent of planks, in which the owner sleeps, while his woodmen lie about in the open air when they are not paddling the raft and guiding it down the stream. These rafts come down the Dvina and its feeders for a thousand miles. Cut in the great forests of Vologda and Nijni Konets, the pines are dragged to the waterside, and knitted by rude hands into these broad, floating masses. At the towns some sturdy helpers may be hired for nothing; many of the poor peasants being anxious to get down the river on their way to the shrines of Solovetsk. For a passage on the raft these pilgrims take a turn at the oar, and help the owners to guide her through the shoals.

In the praams the life is a little less bleak and rough than it is on board the rafts. In form the praam is like the toy called a Noah's ark; a huge hull of coarse pine-logs, riveted and clamped with iron, covered by a peaked plank roof. A big one will cost from six to seven hundred rubles (the ruble may be reckoned for the moment as half-a-crown), and will carry from six to eight hundred tons of oats and rye. A small section of the praam is boarded off to be used as a room. Some bits of pine are shaped into a stool, a table, and a shelf. From the roof-beam swings an iron pot, in which the boatmen cook their food while they are out in the open stream; at other times—that is to say, when they are lying in port—no fire is allowed on board, not even a pipe is lighted, and the watermen's victuals must be cooked on shore. Four or five logs lashed together serve them for a launch, by means of which they can easily paddle to the bank.

Like the rafts, these praams take on board a

great many pilgrims from the upper country; giving them a free passage down, with a supply of tea and black bread as rations, in return for their labour at the paddle and the oar. Not much labour is required, for the praam floats down with the stream. Arrived at Archangel, she empties her cargo of oats into the foreign ships (most of them bound for the Forth, the Tyne, and the Thames); and then she is moored to the bank, cut up, and sold. Some of her logs may be used again for building sheds, the rest is of little use, except for the kitchen and the stove.

The new port of Archangel (called Solambola) is a scattered handful of log-houses, that would remind you of a Swiss hamlet were it not for the cluster of green cupolas and spires, reminding you still more strongly of a Bulgarian town. Each belfry bears a crescent, crowned by a cross. Along the brink of the river runs a strand, some six or eight feet above the level plain; beyond this strand, the fields fall off, so that the country might be laid under water, while the actual strand stood high and dry. The new port is a water-village; for in the spring-time, when the ice is melting up stream, the flood goes over all, and people have to pass from house to magazine in boats.

Not a grain of this strand in front of the sheds is Russ; the whole line of road being built of ballast, brought into the Dvina by foreign ships, and chiefly from English ports. This ridge of pebble, marl, and shells, comes nearly all from London, Liverpool, and Leith; the Russian trade with England having this peculiarity, that it is wholly an export trade. A Russian sends us everything he has for sale; his oats, his flax, his deals, his mats, his furs, his tar; he buys either nothing, or next to nothing, in return. A little salt and wine, a few saw-mills— chiefly for foreign account—are what come back from England by way of barter with the North. The payment is gold, the cargo ballast; and the balance of account between the two countries is—a strand of English marl and shells.

CHAPTER IV.

Archangel.

On passing up the Dvina from the Polar sea, your first experience shows that you are sailing from the West into the East.

When scraping the bar, you notice that the pilot refuses to drop his lead. "Never mind," he says, "it is deep enough; we shall take no harm; unless it be the will of God." A pilot rarely throws out his line. The regulation height of water on the bar is so and so; and dropping a rope into the sea will not, he urges, increase the depth.

When climbing through the delta, you observe that every peasant on the shore, both man and woman, wears a sheepskin wrap; the garment of nomadic tribes; not worn as a rule by any of the settled races on the earth.

In catching a first glimpse of the city, you are struck by the forest of domes and spires; the domes all colour and the spires all gold; a cluster of sacred buildings, you are apt to fancy, out of all proportion to the number of people dwelling in the town.

On feeling for the river-side, a captain finds no quay, no dock, no landing-pier, no stair. He brings-to as he can; and drags his boat into position with a pole, as he would have to do in the Turkish ports of Vidin and Rustchuk. No help is given him from the shore. Except in some ports of Palestine, you will nowhere find a wealthy trade conducted by such simple means.

When driving up that strand of English marl, towards the city of which you see the golden lights, you hear that in Archangel, as in Aleppo, there is no hotel; not even, as in Aleppo, a public khan.

Full of these signs, you turn to your maps, and notice that Archangel lies a little to the east of Mecca and Trebizond.

Yet these highways of the Dvina are not those of the genuine East. Baksheesh is hardly known. Your pilot may sidle up, and give your hand a squeeze (all Russians of the lower ranks are fond of squeezing!) on your safe arrival in the port; and if you fail to take his hint, as probably you will, he whispers meekly in your ear, as though he were telling you an important secret, that very few strangers come into the Dvina, but those few never fail to reward with na-chai (tea-money) the man who has brought them in from the sea of storms. But from the port officials, nothing can be got by giving vails in the bad old way. Among the many wise things which have been done in the present reign, is that of reducing the number of men employed in the customs, and of largely increasing the salaries paid to them by the crown. No man is now underpaid for the service he has to do, and no one in the customs is allowed to accept a bribe. Prince Obolenski, chief of this great department, is a man of high courage as well as high principles, and under his eye the service has been purged of those old abuses which caused it to be branded with black and red in so many books. One case came under my notice, in which a foreign skipper had given to an officer in the port a dozen oranges; not as a bribe, but as a treat; oranges being rarely seen in this northern clime. Yet, when the fact was found out by his local superior, the man was reduced from a high post in the service to a low one. "If he will take an orange, he will take a ruble," said his chief; and a year elapsed before the offender was restored to his former grade.

The new method is not so Asiatic as the old; but in time, it will lead the humblest officer in Russia to feel that he is a man.

Archangel is not a port and city in the sense in which Hamburg and Hull are ports and cities; clusters of docks and sheds, with shops, and waggons, and a busy private trade. Archangel is a camp of shanties, heaped around groups of belfries, cupolas and domes. Imagine a vast green marsh along the bank of a broad brown river, with mounds of clay cropping here and there out of the peat and bog; put buildings on these mounds of clay; adorn the buildings with frescoes, crown them with cupolas and crosses; fill in the space between church and convent, convent and church, with piles and planks, so as to make ground for gardens, streets, and yards; cut two wide lanes, from the church called Smith's Wife to the monastery of St. Michael, three or four miles in length; connect these lanes and the stream by a dozen clearings; paint the walls of church and convent white, the domes green and blue; surround the log-houses with open gardens; stick a geranium, a fuschia, an oleander into every window; leave the grass growing everywhere in street and clearing,—and you have Archangel.

Half-way from Smith's Wife's quarter to the Monastery, stand, in picturesque groups, the sites determined by the mounds of clay, the public buildings; fire-tower, cathedral, town-hall, court of justice, governor's house, museum; new and rough, with a glow of bright new paint upon them all. The collection in the museum is poor; the gilt on the cathedral rich. When seen from a distance, the domes and turrets of Archangel give it the appearance of some sacred Eastern city rather than a place of trade.

This seaport on the Dvina is the only port in Russia proper. Astrachan is a Tartar port; Odessa, an Italian port; Riga, a Livonian port; Helsingfors, a Finnish port. None of these outlets to the sea are in Russia proper, nor is the language spoken in any of them Russ. Won by the sword, they may be lost by the sword. As foreign conquests, they must follow the fate of war; and in Russia proper their loss might not be deeply felt; Great Russia being vast enough for independence and rich enough for happiness, even if she had to live without that belt of lesser Russias in which for her pride and punishment she has lately been clasped and strained. Archangel, on the other side, is her one highway to the sea; the outlet of her northern waters; her old and free communication with the world; an outlet given to her by God, and not to be taken away from her by man.

Such as they are, the port and city of Archangel owe their birth to English adventure, their prosperity to English trade.

In the last year of King Edward the Sixth, an English ship, in pressing her prow against the sandbanks of the Frozen Sea, hoping to light on a passage to Cathay, met with a broad sheet of water, flowing steadily and swiftly from the South. That ship was the "Bonaventure;" her master was Richard Challoner; who had parted from his chief, Sir Hugh Willoughby, in a storm. The water coming down from the south was fresh. A low green isle lay on his port, which he laid down in his chart as Rose Island; afterwards to be famous as the cradle of our northern trade. Pushing up the stream in search of a town, he came upon a small cloister, from the monks of which he learned that he was not in Cathay, but in Great Russia.

Great was a name given by old Russians, not only to the capital of their country, but to the country itself. Their capital was Great Novgorod; their country was Great Russia.

Sir Hugh Willoughby was driven by storms into "the harbour of death," in which he and his crews all perished in the ice; while his luckier lieutenant pushed up the Dvina to Vologda, whence he forced his way to Moscow, and saw the Grand Duke, Ivan the Fourth. In that age Russia was known to Europe as Moscovia, from the city of Moscow; a city which had ravaged her old pre-eminence from Novgorod, and made herself mistress of the Northern Coasts.

Challoner was wrecked and drowned on his second voyage; but those who followed him built an English factory for trade on Rose Island, near the cloister; while the Russians, on their side, built a fort and town on the Dvina, some thirty miles from its mouth; in which position they could watch the strangers in their country, and exchange with them their wax and skins for cotton shirts and pewter pans. The builder of this fort and town was Ivan Vassilivitch, known to us as Ivan the Terrible—Ivan the Fourth.

Ivan called his town the New Castle of St. Michael the Archangel; an unwieldy name, which his raftmen and sailors soon cut down—as raftmen and sailors will—into the final word. On English lips the name would have been St. Michael; but a Russian shrinks from using the name of that prince of heaven. To him Michael is not a saint, as Nicolas and George are saints; but a Power, a Virtue, and a Sanctity, before whose lance the mightiest of rebel angels fell. No Russian speaks of this celestial warrior as a saint. He is the Archangel; greatest of the Host; selected Champion of the living God. Convents and churches are inscribed to him by his celestial rank; but never by his personal name. The great cathedral of Moscow is only known as the Archangel's church. Michael is understood; for who but Michael could be meant? Ivan Vassilivitch had such a liking for this fighting

Power, that on his death-bed he gave orders for his body to be laid, not in that splendid pile of St. Vassili, which he had spent so much time and money in building near the Holy Gate, but in a chapel of the Archangel's church; and there the grim old tyrant lies, in a plain stone coffin, covered with a velvet pall.

Peter the Great rebuilt Archangel on a larger scale with more enduring brick. Peter was fond of the Frozen Sea, and twice, at least, he sailed over it to pray in the convent of Solovetsk; a place which he valued, not only as a holy shrine, but as a frontier fortress, held by his brave old Russ against the Lapps and Swedes. Archangel was made by Peter his peculiar care; and masons were fetched from Holland to erect his lines of bastions, magazines, and quays. A castle rose from the ground on the river bank; an island was reclaimed from the river and trimmed with trees; a summer palace was designed and built for the Tsar. A fleet of ships was sent to command the Dvina mouth. In fact, Archangel was one of the three sites—St. Petersburg and Taganrog being the other two—on which the Emperor designed to build cities that, unlike Novgorod and Moscow, should be at once fortresses and ports.

The city of Ivan and the city of Peter have each in turn gone by. Not a stone of Ivan's town remains; for his new castle and monastery, being built of logs, were duly rotted by rain and consumed by fire. A fort and a monastery still protect and adorn the place; but these have both been raised in more recent years. Of Peter's city, though it seemed to be solid as the earth itself, hardly a house is standing to show the style. A heap of arches, riven by frost and blackened by smoke, is seen on the Dvina bank; a pretty kiosk peeps out from between the birches on Moses Isle; and these are all!

In our Western eyes Archangel may seem to be over rich in domes, as the delta may appear to be over rich in crosses; but then, in our Western eyes, the city is a magazine of oats and tar, of planks and skins; while in native eyes it is the Archangel's house, the port of Solovetsk, and the Gate of God.

CHAPTER V.

Religious Life.

A FRIEND is one day driving me from house to house in Archangel, making calls, when we observe from time to time a smart officer going into courtyards.

"This man appears to be dogging our steps."

"Ha!" laughs my friend; "that fellow is an officer of police."

"Why is he following us?"

"He is not following us; he is going his rounds; he is warning the owners of all good houses that four candles must be lighted in each front window to-night at eight o'clock."

"Four candles! For what?"

"The Emperor. You know it is his Angel's Day; you will see the streets all lighted—by police suggestion—at the proper time."

"Surely the police have no need to interfere. The Emperor is popular; and who can forget that this is St. Alexander's Day?"

"There you are wrong; our people hardly know the court at all. You see these shops are open, yon stalls are crowded, that mill is working, as they would be on the commonest day in all the year. A mujik cares but little for kings and queens; he only knows his own Angel—his peculiar saint. If you would test his reverence, ask him to make a coat, repair a tarantass, or fetch in wood, on his Angel's Day. He would rather die at your feet than sully such a day with work. In fact, a mujik is not a courtier—he is only a religious man."

My friend is right in the main, though his illustration takes me as a stranger by surprise.

The first impulse in a Russian heart is duty to God. It is an impulse of observance and respect; at once moral and ceremonial; an impulse with an inner force and an outer form; present in all ranks of society, and in all situations of life; in an army on the march, in a crowd at a country fair, in a lecture-room full of students; showing itself in a princess dancing at a ball, in a huckster writing at his desk, in a peasant tugging at his cart, in a burglar rioting on his spoil.

This duty adorns the land with fane and altar, even as it touches the individual man with penitential grace. Every village must have its shrine, as every child must have his guardian angel and baptismal cross. The towns are rich in churches and convents, just as the citizens are rich in spiritual gifts. I counted twenty spires in Kargopol, a city of two thousand souls. Moscow is said to have four hundred and thirty churches and chapels; Kief, in proportion to her people, is no less rich. All public events are celebrated by the building of a church. In Kief, St. Andrew's Church commemorates the visit of an Apostle; St. Mary's, the introduction of Christianity. In Moscow, St. Vassili's commemorates the conquest of Kazan; the Donskoi Convent, Fedor's victory over the Crim Tartars; St. Saviour's, the expulsion of Napoleon. In Petersburg, St. Alexander's commemorates the first victory won by Russians over Swedes; St. Isaac's, the birth of Peter the Great; Our Lady of Kazan's, the triumphs of Russian arms against the Persian, Turk, and Frank. Where we should build a bridge, the Russians raise a House of God; so that their political and social history is brightly written in their sacred piles.

By night and day, from his cradle to his grave, a Russian lives, as it were, with God; giving up to His service an amount of time and money which no one ever dreams of giving in the West. Like his Arabian brother, the Slavonian is a religious being; and the gulf which separates such men from the Saxon and the Gaul is broader than a reader who has never seen an Eastern town will readily picture to his mind.

An Oriental is a man of prayer. He seems to live for heaven and not for earth; and even in his commonest acts, he pays respect to what he holds to be a celestial law. One hand is clean, the other unclean. One cup is lawful, another cup is unlawful. If he rises from his couch a prayer is on his lips; if he sits down to rest a blessing is in his heart. When he buys and when he sells, when he eats and when he drinks, he remembers that the Holy One is nigh. If poor in purse he may be rich in grace; his cabin a sanctuary, his craft a service, his daily life an act of prayer.

Enter into a Russian shed—you find a chapel. Every room in that shed is sanctified; for in every room there is a sacred image, a domestic altar, and a household god. The inmate steps into that room with reverence; standing for a moment at the threshold, baring his head, crossing himself, and uttering a saintly verse. Once in the house he feels himself in the Presence, and every act of his life is dedicated to Him in whom we live and move. "Slava Bogu"—Glory to God—is a phrase for ever on his lips; not as a phrase only; to be uttered in a light vein, as a formal act, but with an inward bending and confession of the soul. He fasts very much, and pays a respect beyond our measure to sacred places and to sacred things. He thinks day and night of his Angel; and payments are made by him at church for prayers to be addressed in his name to that Guardian Spirit. He finds a divine enjoyment in the sound of cloister-bells, a foretaste of heaven in kneeling near the bones of saints. The charm of his life is a profound conviction of his own unworthiness in the sight of God, and no mere pride of rank ever robs him of the hope that some one higher in virtue than himself will prove his advocate at the throne of grace. He feels a rapture, strange to a Frank, in the cadence of a psalm, and the taste of consecrated bread is to him a fearful joy. Such things are to him not only things of life and death, but of the everlasting life and the everpresent death.

The church is with a Russian early and late. A child is hardly considered as born into the world, until he has been blessed by the pope and made by him a "servant of God."

As the child begins, so he goes on. The cross which he receives in baptism—which he receives in his cradle, and carries to his grave—is but a sign. Religion goes with him to his school, his play-ground, and his workshop. Every act of his life must begin with supplication and end with thanks. A school has a set of prayers for daily use; with forms to be used on commencing a term, on parting for holidays, on engaging a new teacher, on opening a fresh course. It is the same with boys who work in the mill and on the farm. Every one has his office to recite and his fast to keep. The fasting is severe; and more than half the days in a Russian year are days of fasting and humiliation. During the seven weeks before Easter, no flesh, no fish, no milk, no eggs, no butter, can be touched. For five or six weeks before St. Peter's Day, and for six weeks before Christmas Day, no flesh, no milk, no eggs, no butter, can be used. For fifteen days in August, a fast of great severity is held in honour of the Virgin's death. A man must fast on every Wednesday and Friday throughout the year; eating nothing save fish. Besides keeping these public fasts, a man should fast the whole week before making his confession and receiving his sacrament; abstaining from every dainty, from sugar, cigarettes, and everything cooked with fire.

On the eve of Epiphany—the day for blessing the water—no one is suffered to eat or drink until the blessing has been given, about four o'clock, when the consecrated water may be sipped and dinner must be eaten with a joyful heart. To fetch away the water, people carry into church their pots and pans, their jacks and urns; each peasant with a taper in his hand, which he lights at the holy fire, and afterwards burns before his Angel until it dies.

Every new house in which a man lives, every new shop which he opens for trade, must be blessed. A man who moves from one lodging to another must have his second lodging purified by religious rites. Ten or twelve times a-year, the parish priest, attended by his reader and his deacon, enters into every house in his district, sprinkles the rooms with holy water, cleanses them with prayer, and signs them with the cross.

In his marriage, on his dying bed, the Church is with a Russ even more than at his birth and baptism. Marriage, held to be a sacrament, and poetically called a man's coronation, is a long and intricate affair, consisting of many offices, most of them perfect in symbolism as they are lovely in art. Prayers are recited, rings exchanged, and blessings invoked; after which the ceremony is performed; an actual circling of the brows with a golden rim. "Ivan, Servant of God," cries the pope, as he puts the circlet on his brows, "is crowned with Nadia, handmaid of God." The bride is crowned with Ivan, Servant of God.

Some people wear their bridal crowns for a week, then put them back into the sacristy, and obtain a blessing in exchange. Religion touches the lowliest life with a passing ornament. The bride is always a queen, the groom is always a king, on their wedding day.

A man's Angel is with him early and late; a spirit with whom he dares not trifle; one whom he can never deceive. He puts a picture of this Angel in his bedroom, over the pillow on which he sleeps. A light should burn before that picture day and night. The Angel has to be propitiated by prayers, recited by a consecrated priest. His day must be strictly kept, and no work done, except works of charity, from dawn to dusk. A feast must be spread, the family and kindred called under one roof, presents made to domestics and alms dispensed to the poor. On his Angel's day a man must not only go to church, but buy from the priests some consecrated loaves, which he must give to servants, visitors, and guests. On that day he should send for his parish priest, who will bring his gospel and cross, and say a prayer to the Angel, for which he must be paid a fee according to your means. A child receives his Angel's name in baptism, and this Angelic name he can never change. A peasant who was tried in the district court of Moscow on a charge of having forged a passport and changed his name, in order to pass for another man, replied that such a thing could not be done. "How," he asked, in wonder, "could I change my name? I should lose my Angel. I only forged my place of birth."

So closely have religious passions passed into social life, that civil rights are made to depend in no slight degree on the performance of religious duties. Every man is supposed to attend a weekly mass, and to confess his sins, and take a sacrament once a-year. A man who neglects these offices forfeits his civil rights; unless, as sometimes happens in the best of cities, he can persuade his pope to give him a certificate of his exemplary attendance in the parish church!

CHAPTER VI.

Pilgrims.

Next to his religious energy, the mastering passion of a Russ is the untameable craving of his heart for a wandering life.

All Slavonic tribes are more or less fond of roving to and fro; of peddling, and tramping, and seeing the world; of living, as it were, in tents, as the patriarchs lived: but the propensity to ramble from place to place is keener in the Russ than it is in the Bohemian and the Serb.

A while ago the whole of these Slavonic tribes were still nomadic; a people of herdsmen, driving their flocks from plain to plain, in search of grass and water; camping in either tents of skin or in frames of wood not much more solid than tents of skin; carrying with them their wives and children, their weapons of war, and their household gods. They chased the wild game of their country, and when the wild game failed them, they ate their flocks. Some few among them tilled the soil, but only in a crude and fitful way—as an Adouan tends his patch of desert, as a Pawnee trifles with his stretch of plain; for the Slavonic husbandman was nearly as wild a wanderer as the driver of kine and goats. His fields were so vast, his kin so scattered, that the soil which he cropped was of no more value to him than the water he crossed, the air he breathed. He never dreamt of occupying his piece of ground after it had ceased to yield him, in the unbought bounty of nature, his easy harvest of oats and rye.

Some trace of these wandering habits may still be found; especially in the Pilgrim bands.

These Pilgrim bands are not a rabble of children and women, gay and empty folk, like those you meet when the vintage is gathered in Sicily and the south of France; mummers who take to the pilgrim's staff in wantonness of heart, and end a week of devotion by a feast in the auberge and a dance under the plaintain leaves. At best that French or Sicilian rabble is but a spent tradition and a decaying force. But these Northern Pilgrims are grave and sad in their doings, even as the north is grave and sad. You never hear them laugh; you rarely see them smile; their movements are sedate; the only radiance on their life is the light of prayer and praise. Seeing these worshippers in many places and at many times—before the tomb of Sergie near Moscow, and before the manger at Bethlehem, I have everywhere found them the same in reverence, in humility, in steadfastness of soul. One of these lowly Russ surprised me on the Jordan at Bethabara; and only yesterday I helped his brother to cross the Dvina on his march from Solovetsk. The first Pilgrim had visited the tombs of Palestine, from Nazareth to Marsaba; the second, after toiling through a thousand miles of road and river to Solovetsk, is now on his way to the shrines at Kief. As my horses rattled down the Dvina bluffs I saw this humble Pilgrim on his knees, his little pack laid by, and his forehead bent upon the ground in prayer. He was waiting at the ford for some one to come by—some one who could pay the boatman, and would give him a passage on the raft. The day had not yet dawned; the wind came up the river in gusts and chills; yet the face of that lowly man was good to see; a soft and tender countenance, shining with an inward light, and glad with unearthly peace. The world was not much with him, if one might judge from his sackcloth garb, his broken jar, his crust of black bread; but one could not help thinking, as he bowed in thanks, that it might be well for some of us, who wear fine linen and dine off dainty food, to be even as that poor Pilgrim was.

This pilgrimage to the tombs and shrines of Russian saints, so far from being a holiday adventure, made when the year is spent and the season of labour past, is to the Pilgrim a thing of life and death. He has degrees. A Pilgrim perfect in his calling will go from shrine to shrine for several years; if God is good to him, he will strive, after making the round of his native shrines, to reach the valley of Nazareth and the heights of Bethlehem and Zion. Some hundreds of these Russian Pilgrims annually achieve this highest effort of the Christian life on earth; making their peace with Heaven by kissing the stones in front of the Redeemer's tomb. Of course the poorer and weaker man can never expect to reach this point of grace; but his native soil is holy; Russia is a land of saints; and his

map is dotted with sacred tombs, to which it is
better for him to toil than rest at home in his sloth
and sin.

These Pilgrims go on foot, in bands of fifty or
sixty persons, men, women, children, each with a
staff in his hand, a water-bottle hanging from his
belt; edifying the country as they march along,
kneeling at the wayside chapel, and singing their
canticles by day and night. The children whine a
plaintive little song, of which the burden runs:

> "Fatherkins and motherkins,
> Give us bread to eat;"

and this appeal of the children is always heard,
since all poor people fancy that the knock of a
Pilgrim at their window may be that of an angel,
and will bring them luck.

A part—a very large part—of these rovers are
simple tramps, who make a trade of piety; carrying
about with them relics and rags which they vend
at high rates to servant girls and superstitious
crones.

A man who in other days would have followed
his sheep and kine, now seeks a wild sort of freedom
as a pilgrim, hugging himself on his immunity from
tax and rent, from wife and brat; migrating from
province to province; a beggar, an impostor, and a
tramp; tickled by the greeting of young and old as
he passes their door, "Whither, O friend, is the Lord
leading thee?" Sooner or later such a man falls in
with a band of pilgrims, which he finds it his good
to join. The Russian Autolycus slings a water-bottle

at his belt, and his female companion limps along the forest road on her wooden staff. You meet them on every track; you find them in the yard of every house. They creep in at back-doors, and have an assortment of articles for sale, which are often as precious in the eyes of a mistress as in those of her maid; a bit of rock from Nazareth, a drop of water from Jordan, a thread from the seamless coat, a chip of the genuine cross. These are the bolder spirits; but thousands of such vagrants roam about the country; telling crowds of gapers what they have seen in some holy place, where miracles are daily performed by the bones of saints. They show you a cross from Troitsa; they give you a morsel of consecrated bread from St. George. They can describe to you the defence of Solovetsk, and tell you of the incorruptible corpses of Pechersk.

These are the impostors—rank and racy impostors—yet some of these men and women who pass you on the roads are pious and devoted souls, wandering about the earth in search of what they fancy is a higher good. A few may be rich; but riches are dust in the eyes of God; and in seeking after His glory they dare not trust to an arm of flesh. Equally with his meekest brother, the rich Pilgrim must take his staff, and march on foot, joining his brethren in their devotions and confessions, in their matins and their evening song.

Most of these Pilgrim bands have to beg their crust of black bread, their sup of sour quass, from people as poor as themselves in money, and almost

as rich in the gifts of faith. Like the hadji going to
Mecca, a Pilgrim coming to Archangel, on his way
to the shrines, is a holy man, with something of the
character of a pope. The peasant, who thinks the
crossing of his door-step by the stranger brings him
blessings, not only lodges him by night, but helps
him on the road by day. A Pilgrim is a sacred
being in rustic eyes. If his Elder would let him
go, he would join the band; but if he may not
wend in person, he will go in spirit, to the shrine.
A prayer shall be said in his name by the monks,
and he will send his last kopek in payment for
that prayer by the hand of this ragged Pilgrim, confident that the fellow would rather die than abuse
his trust.

The men who escape from Siberian mines put
on the pilgrim frock and seize the pilgrim staff.
Thus robed and armed, a man may get from Perm
to Archangel with little risk, even though his flesh
may be burnt and his papers forged. Pietrowski
has told the story of his flight, and many such tales
may be heard on the Dvina praams.

A peasant, living in a village near Archangel,
killed his father in a quarrel, but in such a way
that he was not suspected of the crime; and he
would never have been brought to justice had not
Vanka, a friend and neighbour, been a witness of
the deed. Now Vanka was weak and superstitious,
and every day as he passed the image of his Angel
in the street, he felt an inner yearning to tell what
he had seen. The murderer, watching him day and
night, observed that he prayed very much, and

crossed himself very often, as though he were deeply troubled in his mind. On asking what ailed him, he heard to his alarm that Vanka could neither eat nor sleep while that terrible secret lay upon his soul. But what could he do? Nothing; absolutely nothing? Yes; he could threaten to do for him what he had done by accident for a better man. "Listen to me, Vanka," he said, in a resolute tone; "you are a fool; but you would not like to have a knife in your throat, would you?" "God take care of me!" cried Vanka. "Mind me, then," said the murderer: "if you prate, I will have your blood." Vanka was so much frightened that he went to the police that very night, and told them all he knew; on which his friend was arrested, brought to trial in Archangel, and condemned to labour on the public works for life. Vanka was the main witness, and on his evidence the judge pronounced his sentence. Then a scene arose in court, which those who saw it say they shall not forget. The man in the dock was bold and calm, while Vanka, his accuser, trembled from crown to sole; and when the sentence of perpetual exile to the mines was read, the murderer turned to his friend and said, in a clear, firm voice, "Vanka! remember my words. To-day is yours: I am going to Siberia; but I shall come to your house again, and then I shall take your life. You know!" Years went by, and the threat, forgotten by every one else, was only remembered by Vanka, who, knowing his old friend too well, expected each passing night would be his last on earth. At length the tragedy came in a ghastly form. Vanka was found dead in his bed; his throat was cut from ear to ear; and in a drinking-den close by lay his murderer, snoring in his cups. He had made his escape from the mines; he had traversed the whole length of Asiatic Russia; he had climbed the Ural chain; and walked through the snow and ice of Perm; travelling in a Pilgrim's garb, and singing the Pilgrim's song, until he came to the suburbs of Archangel, where he slipped away from his raft, hid himself in the wood until night-fall, crept to the familiar shed, and drew his knife across Vanka's throat.

No one suspects a Pilgrim. With a staff in his hand, a sheepskin on his back, a water-bottle at his belt, and a clot of bass tied loosely round his feet, a peasant of the Ural mountains quits his home, and makes no merit of trudging his two or three thousand miles. On the river he takes an oar, on the wayside he endures with incredible fortitude the burning sun by day, the biting frost at night. In Moscow, I heard the history of three sisters, born in that city, who have taken up the Pilgrim's staff for life. They are clever women, milliners by trade, and much employed by ladies of high rank. If they could only rest in their shop, they might live in comfort, and end their days in peace. But the religious and nomadic passions of their race are strong upon them. Every year they go to Kief, Solovetsk, and Jerusalem; and the journey occupies them forty-nine weeks. Every year, they spend three weeks at home, and then set out again; alone, on foot; to seek, in winter snow and summer heat, salvation for their souls. No force on earth—save that which drives an Arab across the desert, and a Mormon across the prairie—is like this force.

In the hope of seeing these pilgrim bands, of going with them to Solovetsk, and studying them on the spot,—as also of inquiring about the Convent Spectre, and solving the mystery which for many years past connected that spectre with the Romanof family,—I rounded the North Cape, and my regret is deep, when landing at Archangel, to hear that the last Pilgrim band has sailed, and that no more boats will cross the Frozen Sea until the ice breaks up in May next year.

CHAPTER VII.

Father John.

STUNG by this news of the Pilgrim boat having sailed, and haunting, unquietly, the Pilgrims' Court in the upper town, I notice a good many sheepskin garbs, with wearers of the burnt and hungry sort you meet in all seasons on the Syrian roads. They are exceedingly devout, and even in their rags and filth they have a certain grace of aspect and of mien. A pious purpose seems to inform their gestures and their speech. Yon poor old man going home with his morsel of dried fish, has the air of an Arab sheikh. These Pilgrims, like myself, have been detained by storms; and a hope shoots up into my heart, that as the monks must either send away all these thirsty souls unslaked, or lodge and feed them for several months, they may yet contrive to send a boat.

A very small monk, not five feet high, with girl-like hair and rippling beard, which parts and flows out wildly in the wind, is standing in the gate-way of the Pilgrims' Court; and hardly knowing how it might be best to put the matter in my feeble Russ, I ask him in that tongue where a man should look for the Solovetsk boat.

"English?" inquires the girl-like monk.

"Yes; English," I reply, in some surprise; having

never before seen a monk in Russia who could speak in any other tongue than Russ. "The boat," he adds, "has ceased to run; and is now at Solovetsk laid up in dock."

In dock! This dwarf must be a wag; for such a conjunction as monks and docks in a country where you find a quay like that of Solambola is, of course, a joke. "In dock!"

"Oh, yes, in dock."

"Then have you a dock in the Holy Isle?"

"A dock—why not? The merchants of Archangel have no docks, you say! Well, that is true; but merchants are not monks. You see, the monks of Solovetsk labour while the merchants of Archangel trade. Slava Bogu! a good monk does his work; no shuffling and no waste. In London you have docks?"

"Yes, many; but they were not built by monks."

"In England, you have no monks; once you had them; and then they built things—eh?"

This dwarf is certainly a wag. What, monks who work, and docks in the Frozen Sea! After telling me where he learned his English (which is of nautical and naughty pattern), the manikin comforts me with news that although the Pilgrim boat has gone back to Solovetsk (where her engines are to be taken out, and put by in warm boxes near a stove for the winter months)—a provision-boat may sail for the monastery in about a week.

"Can you tell me where to find the captain of that boat?"

"Hum!" says the dwarf, slowly, crossing himself the while, and lipping his silent prayer, "*I am the skipper!*"

My surprise is great. This dwarf, in a monk's gown and cap, with a woman's auburn curls, the captain of a sea-going ship! On a second glance at his slight figure, I notice that his eyes are bright, that his cheek is bronze, that his teeth, though small, are bony and well set. In spite of his serge gown and his girl-like face, there *is* about the tiny monk that look of mastery which becomes the captain of a ship.

"And can you give me a passage in your boat?"

"You! English, and you wish to see the holy tombs? Well, that is something new. No men of your nation ever sail to Solovetsk. They come over here to buy, and not to pray. Sometimes they come to fight."

The last five words, spoken in a low key, come out from between his teeth, with a snap, which is highly comic in a man so lowly and so small. A lady living at Onega told me some days ago, that once, when she was staying for a week at Solovetsk, with a Russian party, she was compelled to hide her English birth, from fear lest the monks should kill her. A woman's fancy, doubtless; but her words come back upon my mind, with a very odd sort of start, as the manikin knits his brow and hisses at the English fleet.

"Where is your boat? and what is she called?"

"She lies in the lower port, by the Pilgrims'

Wharf; her name is the Vera; as you would say, the Faith."

"How do you call your captain?" I inquire of a second monk, who is evidently a sailor also; in fact, he is the first mate, serving on board the Faith.

"Ivan," says the monk; a huge fellow, with hasty eyes and audacious front; "but we mostly call him Vanoushka, because he is little and because we like him." Vanoushka is one of the affectionate forms of Ivan: Little Ivan, Little John. The skipper, then, is properly Father John.

As for the next ten days and nights we are to keep company, it may be best for me to say at once what I came to know of the queer little skipper in the long gown and with the woman's curls.

Father John is an infant of the soil. Born in a Lapland village, he had before him from his cradle the hard and hopeless life of a woodman and codfisher, the two trades carried on by all poor people in these countries, where the modes of life are fixed by the climate and the soil. In the summer he would cut logs and grass; in the winter he would hunt the sea in search of seal and cod. But the lad was smart and lively; he wished to see the world, and hoped in some future time to sail a boat of his own. In order to rise he must learn; in order to become a skipper he must study the art of guiding ships at sea. Some thirty miles from the hamlet where he lived stood Kem, an ancient town established on the Lapland coast by colonists from Novgorod the Great, in which town there was a school of navigation; rude and simple as became so poor a place; but better than none at all, and to this provincial school Father John contrived to go. That movement was his first great step in life.

From Kem you can see a group of high and wooded islands towards the rising sun, the shores of which shine with a peculiar light in the early dawn. They seem to call you, as it were by a spell, into some paradise of the north. Every view is green, and every height is crowned by a church with a golden cross. These islands are the Solovetsk group; and once, at least, the lad went over from Kem in a boat to pray in that holy place. The lights, the music, and the ample cheer, appealed to his fancy and his stomach; leaving on his mind an impression of peace and fulness never to be effaced.

He got his pass as a seaman, came over to Archangel, fell into loose ways, and meeting with some German sailors from the Baltic, listened to their lusty songs and merry tales, until he felt a desire to leave his own country and go with them on a voyage. Now sailors are scarce in the Russian ports; the Emperor Nicolas was in those days drafting his seamen into the Black Sea fleets; and for a man to quit Russia without a pass from the police was a great offence. Such a pass the lad felt sure he could never get; and when the German vessel was about to sail he crept on board her in the night, and got away to sea without being found out by the port-police.

The vessel in which he escaped from his country

was the "Hero" of Passenburg, in Hanover, plying as a rule between German and Danish ports, but sometimes running over to the Tyne and the Thames. Entered on the ship's books in a foreign name, Father John adopted the tastes of his new comrades; learned to eat English beef, to drink German beer; and to carry himself like a man of the world. But the teaching of his father and his pope was not lost upon him, even in the slums of Wapping and on the quays of Rotterdam. He began to pine for religion, as a Switzer pines for his Alp and an Egyptian for his Nile. What could he do? The thought of going home to Kem was a fearful dream. The lash, the jail, the mine, awaited him—he thought—in his native land.

Cut off from access to a priest of his own religion, he talked to his fellows before the mast about their faith. Some laughed at him; some cursed him; but one old sailor took him to the house of a Catholic priest. For four or five weeks Father John received a lesson every day in the creed of Rome; but his mind misgave him as to what he heard; and when his vessel left the port he was still without a Church. In the Levant, he met with creeds of all nations—Greek, Italian, Lutheran, Armenian—but he could not choose between them, and his mind was troubled with continual longings for a better life.

Then he was wrecked in the Gulf of Venice, and having nearly lost his life, he grew more and more uneasy about his soul. A few months later he was wrecked on the coast of Norway; and for the second time in one year, he found himself at the gates of death. He could not live without religion; and the only religion to whisper peace to his soul, was that of his early and better days. But then the service of his country is one of strict observance, and a man who cannot go to church cannot exercise his faith. How was he to seek for God in a foreign port?

A chance of coming back to Russia threw itself in his path. The ship in which he served—a German ship—was chartered by an English firm for Archangel, and as Father John was the only Russ on board, the skipper saw that his man would be useful in such a voyage. But the news was to John a fearful joy. He longed to see his country once more, to kneel at his native shrines, to give his mother some money he had saved; but he had now been twelve years absent without leave, and he knew that for such an offence he could be sent to Siberia, as he phrased it, "like a slave." His fear overcame his love, and he answered the skipper that he would not go and must quit the ship.

But the skipper understood his trade. Owing John some sixteen pounds for pay, he told him that he had no money, where he lay, and could not settle accounts until they arrived in Archangel where he would receive his freight. "Money," says the Russ proverb, "likes to be counted;" and when Father John thrust his hands into empty pockets, he began to think, after all, it might be better to go home, to get his wages, and see what would be done.

With a shaven chin and foreign name, he might have kept his secret and got away from Archangel undiscovered by the port-police, had he not yielded the night before he should have sailed, and gone with some Germans of the crew to a drinking den. Twelve years of abstinence from vodka had caused him to forget the power of that evil spirit; he drank too much, he lost his senses; and when he woke next day he found that his mates had left him, that his ship had sailed. What could he do? If he spoke to the German consul, he would be treated as a deserter from his post. If he went to the Russian police, he fancied they would knout him to death. Not knowing what to say, or how to act, he was mooning in the port, when he met an old school-fellow from Kem, one Jacob Kollownoff (whom I afterwards came to know). Like most of the hardy men of Kem, Jacob was prospering in the world; he was a skipper, with a boat of his own, in which he made distant and daring voyages. At the moment when he met Father John, he was preparing for a run to Spitzbergen in search of cod, to be salted at sea, and carried to the markets of Cronstadt. Jacob saw no harm in a sailor drinking a glass too much, and knowing that John was a good hand, he gave him a place in his boat and took him out on his voyage. The cod was caught, and Cronstadt reached; but the return was luckless; and John was cast away for the third time in his life. A wrecked and broken man, he now made up his mind to quit the sea, and even to take his chance of what his people might do with him at home.

Returning to Kem with the skipper, he was seized by the police, on the ground of his papers being out of order, and cast into the common jail of the town, where he lay for twelve months untried. The life in jail was not harder than his life on deck; for the government paid him, as a prisoner, six kopeks a-day; enough to supply his wants. He was never brought before a court. Once, if not more than once, the elder hinted that a little money would make things straight, and he might go his way. The sum suggested as enough for the purpose was seventy-five rubles—nearly ten pounds in English coin. "Tell him," said John to his brother, who brought this message to the jail, "he shall not get from me so much as one kopek."

A week later he was sent in a boat from Kem to Archangel, under sentence, he was told, of two years' hard labour in the fort; but either the elder talked too big or his message was misread, for on going up to the police-office in that city the prisoner was examined and discharged.

A dream of the summer isles and golden pinnacles came back to him; he had lived his worldly life, and longed for rest. Who can wonder that he wished to become a monk of Solovetsk!

To the Convent his skill in seamanship was of instant use. A steamer had just been bought in Glasgow for the carriage of pilgrims to and fro; and on her arrival in Archangel, Feofan, Archimandrite of Solovetsk, discharged her Scottish crew and manned her with his monks. At first these holy men felt strange on deck; they crossed themselves;

they sang a hymn; and as the pistons would not move, they begged the Scottish engineer to return; since the machine—being made by heretics—had not grace enough to obey the voice of a holy man. They made two or three midsummer trips across the gulf, getting hints from the native skippers, and gradually warming to their work. A priest was appointed captain, and monks were sent into the kitchen and the engine-room. All went well for a time; Savatie and Zosima—the local saints of Solovetsk—taking care of their followers in the fashion of St. Nicolas and St. George.

Yet Father John was a real God's gift to the Convent; for the voyage is not often to be described as a summer trip; and even so good a person as an Archimandrite likes to know when he goes down into the Frozen Sea, that his saints are acting through a man who has sailed in the roughest waters of the world.

CHAPTER VIII.

The Vladika.

"You have a letter of introduction to the Archimandrite of Solovetsk?" asks Father John, as we are shaking hands under the Pilgrim's lamp. "No! Then you must get one."

"Why? Are you so formal when a Pilgrim comes to the holy shrines?"

"You are not quite a Pilgrim. You will need a room in the guest-house for yourself. You may wish to have horses, boats, and people to go about. You will want to see the sacristy, the jewels, and the books. You may like to eat at the Archimandrite's board."

"But how are these things to be done?"

"You know the Most Sacred Vladika of Archangel, perhaps?"

"Well, yes, a little." One of the Vladika's closest friends has been talking to me of that Sacred personage, and has promised to present me this very day.

"Get from him a line to the Archimandrite. That will make all things smooth," says Father John.

"Are they great friends?"

"Ha! who can tell? You see, the Most Sacred Vladika used to be master of every one in the

Holy Isles; and now .... but then the Vladika of Archangel and the Archimandrite of Solovetsk are holy men, not likely to fall out. You'll get a line!"

"Yes; if he will give me one; good-bye."

"Count on a week for the voyage, and bring white bread," adds the dwarf. "Prosteté — Pardon me."

Of course, the Vladika (bishop or archbishop) is a monk; for every high-priest in the Orthodox Church, whether his rank be that of vicar, archimandrite, bishop, or metropolite, must wear the hood, and must have taken vows. The rule that a bishop must be "the husband of one wife," is set aside so far as regards the clergy of higher grades. A parish priest is a married man; must, in fact, be a married man; and no young deacon can obtain a church until he has first obtained a bride. The social offices of the Church are done by these family men; baptism, purifying, marriage, confession, burial; yet the higher seats in the hierarchy are all reserved (as yet) for celibates who are under vows.

The Holy Governing Synod—highest court of the Orthodox Church—consists of monks, with one lay member to assist them by his knowledge of the world. No married priest has ever had a seat on that governing board. The Metropolites are monks; and not only monks, but actual rulers of monastic houses. Isidore, metropolite of Novgorod, is archimandrite of the great convent of St. George. Arseny, metropolite of Kief, is archimandrite of the great convent of Pechersk. Innocent, metropolite of Moskow, is archimandrite of the great convent of

Troitsa. All the vicars of these high-priests are monks. The case of Archangel and Solovetsk is, therefore, the exception to a general rule. St. George, Pechersk, and Troitsa, are governed by the nearest prince of the Church; and in former times this was also the case with Solovetsk; but Peter the Great, in one of his fits of reverence, broke this old connexion of the convent and the see of Archangel; endowing the Archimandrite of Solovetsk with a separate standing and an independent power. Some people think the Archbishop of Archangel nurses a grudge against the civil power for this infringement of his ancient rights; and this idea was probably present in the mind of Father John.

Acting on Father John's advice, I put on my clothes of state—a plain dress suit; the only attire in which you can wait on a man of rank—and drive to my friend's abode, and finding him ready to go with me, gallop through a gust of freezing rain to the palace-door.

The Archbishop is at home, though it is not yet twelve o'clock. It is said of him that he seldom goes abroad; affecting the airs of an exile and a martyr; but doing—in a sad, submissive way, as if the weapon were unworthy of its work—a great deal of good; watching over his church, admonishing his clergy, both white and black, and thinking, like a father, for the poor.

Leaving our wraps in an outer hall (the proper etiquette of guests), we send in our cards by an usher, and are received at once.

The Most Sacred Vladika, pale as a ghost,

dressed in a black gown, on which hangs a sapphire cross, and wearing his hood of serge, rises to greet us; and coming forward with a sweet and vanishing smile, first blesses his penitent, and then shakes hands with his English guest.

This Most Sacred Father Nathaniel is now an aged, shadowy man, with long white beard, and a failing light in his meek blue eyes. But in his prime he is said to have been handsome in person, eager in gait, caressing in style. In his youth, he was a village pastor; one of the White clergy; married, and a family man; but his wife died early; and as a pastor in his church cannot marry a second time, he followed a fashion long ago set by his aspiring brethren—he took the vows of chastity, became a monk, and began to rise. His fine face, his courtly wit, his graceful bearing, brought him hosts of fair penitents, and these fair penitents made for him high friends at court. He was appointed Vicar of St. Petersburg; a post not higher in actual rank than that of a Dean of St. Paul's; but one which a popular and ambitious man prefers to most of the Russian sees. Father Nathaniel was an idol of the city. Fine ladies sought his advice, and women of all classes came to confess to him their sins. Princes fell beneath his sway; princesses adored him; and no rank in the Church, however high, appeared to stand beyond his reach. But these court triumphs were his ruin. He was such a favourite with ladies, that his brethren began to smile with malicious leer when his back was turned, and drop their poisonous hints about the ways in which he walked. They said he was too fond of power; they said he spent more time with his female penitents than became a monk. It is the misery of these vicars and bishops that they cannot be married men, with wives of their own to turn the edges of such shafts. Men's tongues kept wagging against Nathaniel's fame; and even those who knew him to be earnest in his faith, began to think it might be well for the Church if this fascinating Father could be honourably sent to some distant see.

Whither was he to go?

While a place was being sought for him, he happened to give deep offence in high quarters; and as Father Alexander, Vladika of Archangel (hero of Solovetsk), was eager to go south and be near the court, Father Nathaniel was promoted to that hero's place.

He left St. Petersburg amidst the tears of fair women, who could not protect their idol against the malice of envious monks. Taking his promotion meekly, as became his robe, he sighed to think that his day was come, and in the future he would count in his church as a fallen man. Arriving in Archangel, he shut himself up in his palace near the monastery of St. Michael; a house which he found too big for his simple wants. Soon after his coming he abandoned this palace for a smaller house; giving up his more princely pile to the monks of St. Michael for a public school.

A spirit of sacrifice is the pre-eminent virtue of the Russian Church.

The shadowy old man compels me to sit on the

sofa by his side; talks of my voyage round the
North Cape; shows me a copy in Russian of my
book on the Holy Land; inquires whether I know
the Pastor Xatli in London. Fancying that he
means the Russian pope in Welbeck Street, I answer, Yes; on which we get into much confusion of
tongues; until it flashes upon me that he is talking
of Mr. Hatherley of Wolverhampton, the gentleman
who has gone over from the English to the Russian
rite, and is said to have carried some twenty souls
of the Black Country with him. What little there
is to tell of this Oriental church in our Black Country is told; and in return for my scanty supply of
facts, the Vladika is good enough to show me the
pictures hanging on his wall. These pictures are of
two classes, holy and loyal; first the sacred images
—those heads of our Saviour and of the Virgin
Mother, which hang in the corners of every Russian
room, the tutelary presence, to be adored with reverence at the dawn of day and the hour of rest;
then the loyal and local pictures—portraits of the
reigning house, and of former archbishops—which
you would expect to find in such a house; a first
Alexander, with flat and dreamy face; a Nicolas,
with stiff and haughty figure; a second Alexander,
hung in the place of honour, and wearing a pensive
and benignant smile. More to my mind, as less
familiar than these great ones of the hour, is the
fading image of a lady, thoroughly Russ in garb
and aspect—Marfa, boyarine of Novgorod and Co-
lonizer of the North.

Nathaniel marks with kindling eyes my interest

in this grand old creature—builder alike of convents and of towns—who sent out from Novgorod two of her sons, and hundreds of her people, to the bleak north country, then inhabited by pagan Lapps and Karels, worshippers of the thunder-cloud, and children of the Golden Hag. Her story is the epic of these Northern shores.

While Red and White Rose were wasting our English counties with sword and fire, this energetic princess sent her sons and her people down the Volkhoff, into Lake Ladoga, whence they crept up the Swir into Lake Onega; from the banks of which lake they marched upwards, through the forests of birch and pine, into the frozen North. She sent them to explore the woods, to lay down rivers and lakes, to tell the natives of a living God. They came to Holmogory, on the Dvina, then a poor fishing-village occupied by Karels, a tribe not higher in type than the Samoyeds of the present day. They founded Suma, Soroka, and Kem. They took possession of the Frozen Sea and its clustering isles. In dropping down a main arm of the river, Marfa's two sons were pitched from their boat and drowned. Their bodies being washed on shore and buried in the sand, she caused a cloister to be raised on the spot, which she called the Monastery of St. Nicolas, after the patron of drowning men.

That cloister of St. Nicolas was the point first made by Challoner when he entered the Dvina from the Frozen Sea.

"You are going over to Solovetsk?" says the Vladika, coming back to his sofa. "We have no authority in the isles, although they lie within our See. It pleased the Emperor Peter, on his return from a stormy voyage, to raise the Convent of Savatie to independent rank, to give it the title of Lavra—making it the equal, in our ecclesiastical system, with Troitsa, Pechersk, and St. George. From that day Solovetsk became a separate province of the Church, dependent on the Holy Governing Synod and the Tsar. Still I can give you a line to Feofan, the Archimandrite."

Slipping into an inner room for five minutes, he composes a mandate in my favour, in the highest Oriental style.

CHAPTER IX.

A Pilgrim Boat.

A LADY, who knows the country, puts up in a crate such things as a pilgrim may chance to need in a monastic cell—good tea, calf's tongue, fresh butter, cheese, roast beef, and indispensable white bread. These dainties being piled on a drojki, propped on pillows and covered with quilts—my bedding in the convent and the boat—we rattle away to the Pilgrims' Wharf.

Yes, there it is, an actual wharf—the only wharf in Archangel along which boats can lie, and land their passengers by a common sea-side plank!

Moored to the capstan by a rope, lies the pretty craft; a gilt cross on her fore-mast, a saintly pennant on her main. Four large gold letters tell her name:

В Ѣ Р А

(pronounced Verra,) and meaning Faith. Father John is standing on his bridge, giving orders in a low voice to his officers and crew, many of whom are monks—mate, steward, cook, and engineer—each and all arrayed in the cowl and frock.

On the Pilgrims' wharf, which lies in a yard, cut off by gates from the street, and paved with chips and shavings to form a dry approach, stands a new pile of monastic buildings; chapels, cells, storerooms, offices, stalls, dormitories; in fact, a new Pilgrims' Court. A steamer cannot reach the port in the upper town, where the original Pilgrims' Court was built; and the Fathers, keeping pace with the times, have let their ancient lodgings in the town, and built a new house lower down the stream.

Crowds of men and women—pilgrims, tramps, and soldiers—strew the wharf with a litter of baskets, tea-pots, beds, dried-fish, felt boots, old rugs and furs, salt-girkins, black bread; through which the monks step softly and sadly; helping a child to trot on board, getting a free pass for a beggar, buying rye-loaves for a lame wretch, and otherwise aiding the poorest of these poor creatures in their need. For, even though the season is now far spent, nearly two hundred pilgrims are in waiting on the Pilgrims' wharf; all hoping to get over to the Holy Isles. Most of these men have money to pay their fare; and some among the groups are said to be rich. A dozen of the better sort, natives of Archangel, too busy to pass over the sea in June, when their river was full of ships, are taking advantage of the lull in trade, and of the extra boat. Each man brings with him a basket of bread and fish, a box of tea, a thick quilt, and a pair of felt leggings, to be worn over his boots at night. These local pilgrims carry a staff; but in place of the leathern belt and water-bottle, they carry a teapot and a cup. One man wears a cowl and gown, who is not of the crew; a jolly, riotous monk, going back to his convent as a prisoner. "What has he been doing?" "Women and drink," says Father John. The fares are low; first-class, six rubles (fifteen shillings); second-class, four rubles; third-class, three rubles. This tariff covers the cost of going out and coming back—a voyage of four hundred miles—with lodgings in the Guest House, and rations at the common tables, during a stay of five or six days. A dozen of these poor pilgrims have no rubles in their purse, and the question rises on the wharf, whether these paupers shall be left behind. Father John and his fellow-skipper have a general rule; they must refuse no man, however poor, who asks them for a passage to Solovetsk in the name of God.

A bell tolls, a plank is drawn, and we are off. As we back from the wharf, getting clear, a hundred heads bow down, a hundred hands sign the cross, and every soul commends itself to God. Every time that, in dropping down the river, we pass a church, the work of bowing and crossing begins afresh. Each head uncovers; each back is bent; each lip is moved by prayer. Some kneel on deck; some kiss the planks. The men look contrite, and the women are sedate. The crews on fishing-craft salute us; oftentimes kneeling and bowing as we glide past; and always crossing themselves with uncovered heads. Some beg that we will pray for them; and the most worldly sailors pause in their work and hope that the Lord will give us a prosperous wind.

A gale is blowing from west and north. In the river it is not much felt, excepting for the chill, which bites into your bone. Father John, with a monk's contempt for caution, gives the Maimax channel a free berth, and having a boat in hand of very light draught, drops down the ancient arm as a shorter passage into the gulf.

Before we quit the river, our provident worshippers have begun to brew their tea and eat their supper of girkin and black bread.

The distribution on board is simple. Only one passenger has paid the first-class fare. He has the whole state cabin to himself; a room some nine feet square, with bench and mat to sleep on; a cabin in which he might live very well, had it not pleased the monks to stow their winter supply of tallow in the boxes beneath his couch. Two persons have paid the second-class fare; a skipper and his wife, who have been sailing about the world for years, have made their fortunes, and are now going home to Kem. "Ah!" says the fair, fat woman, "you English have a nice country to live in, and you get very good tea; but...." The man is like his wife. "Prefer to live in Kem? Why not? In London you have beef and stout; but you have no summer and no winter; all your seasons are the same; never hot, never cold. If you want to enjoy life, you should drive in a reindeer sledge over a Lapland plain, in thirty degrees of frost."

The rest of our fellow-pilgrims are on deck and in the hold; rich and poor, lame and blind, merchant and beggar, charlatan and saint; a motley group, in which a painter might find models for a Cantwell, a Torquemada, a St. John. You see by their garb, and hear in their speech, that they have come from every province of the Empire; from the Ukraine and from Georgia, from the Crimea and from the Ural heights, from the Gulf of Finland and from the shores of the Yellow Sea. Some of these men have been on foot, trudging through summer sands and winter snows, for more than a year.

The lives of many of my fellow-passengers are like an old wife's tales.

One poor fellow, having no feet, has to be lifted on board the boat. He is clothed in rags; yet this poor pilgrim's face has such a patient look that one can hardly help feeling he has made his peace. He tells me that he lives beyond Viatka, in the province of Perm; that he lost his feet by frost-bite years ago; that he lay sick a long time; that while he was lying in his pain he called on Savatie to help him, promising that saint, on his recovery, to make a pilgrimage to his shrine in the Frozen Sea. By losing his legs, he saved his life; and then, in his poverty and rags, he set forth on his journey, crawling on his stumps, around which he has twisted a coarse leather splinth, over fifteen hundred miles of broken road.

Another pilgrim, wearing a felt boot on one leg, a bass shoe on the other, has a most abject look. He is a drunkard, sailing to Solovetsk to redeem a vow. Lying tipsy on the canal bank at Vietegra, he rolled into the water, and narrowly escaped being drowned. As he lay on his face, the foam oozing slowly from his mouth, he called on his saints to save him, promising them to do a good work in return for such help. To keep that vow he is going to the holy shrines.

A woman is carrying her child, a fine little lad of six or seven years, to be offered to the monks and educated for the cowl. She has passed through trouble; having lost her husband, and her fortune; and she is bent on sacrificing the only gift now left to her on earth. To put her son in the monastery of Solovetsk is to secure him, she believes, against all temporal and all spiritual harm. Poor creature! It is sad to think of her lot when the sacrifice is made, and the lonely woman, turning back from the incense and glory of Solovetsk, has to go once more into the world, and without her child.

An aged man, with flowing beard and priestly mien, though he is wrapped in rags, is noticeable in the groups among which he moves. He is a vowed pilgrim; that is to say, a pilgrim for life, as another man would be a monk for life; his whole time being spent in walking from shrine to shrine. He has the highest rank of a pilgrim; for he has been to Nazareth and Bethlehem, as well as to Novgorod and Kief. This is the third time he has come to Solovetsk; and it is his hope, if God should spare him for the work, to make yet another round of the four most potent shrines, and then lay up his dust in these Holy Isles.

Some of these pilgrims, even those in rags, are bringing gifts of no small value to the Convent fund. Each pilgrim drops his offering into the box; some more, some less, according to his means. Many bear gifts from neighbours and friends who cannot afford the time for so long and perilous a voyage, but who wish to walk with God, and lay up their portion with His saints.

On reaching the river mouth we find a fleet of fishing-boats in dire distress; and the two ships that we passed a week since, bobbing and reeling on the bar like tipsy men, are completely gone. The "Thera" is a Norwegian clipper, carrying deals; the "Olga," a Prussian bark, carrying oats; they are now aground, and raked by the wash from stem to stern. We pass these hulls in prayer; for the gale blows dead in our teeth; and we are only too well aware that before daylight comes again we shall need to be helped by all the spirits that wait on mortal men.

With hood and gown wrapped up in a storm-cape, made for such nights, Father John is standing on his bridge, directing the course of his boat like an English tar. His monks meet the wind with a psalm, in the singing of which the pilgrims and soldiers join. The passenger comes for a moment from his cabin into the sleet and rain; for the voices of these enthusiasts, pealing to the heavens through rack and roar, are like no sounds he has ever yet heard at sea. Many of the singers lie below in the hold; penned up between sacks of rye and casks of grease; some of them deadly sick, some groaning as though their hearts would break; yet more than half these sufferers follow with lifted eyes and strenuous lungs the swelling of that beautiful monkish chant. It is their even-song, and they could not let the sun go down into the surge until that duty to their Maker was said and sung.

Next day there comes no dawn. A man on the bridge declares that the sun is up; but no one else can see it; for a veil of mist droops everywhere about us, out of which comes nothing but a roar of wind and a flood of rain.

The "Faith" is bound to arrive in the Bay of Solovetsk by twelve o'clock; but early in the day, Father John comes to tell me (apart) that he shall not be able to reach his port until five o'clock; and when five is long since past, he returns to tell me, with a patient shrug, that we want more room, and must change our course. The entrance to Solovetsk is through a reef of rocks.

"Must we lie out all night?"

"We must." Two hours are spent in feeling for the shore; Father John having no objection to use his lead. When anchorage is found, we let the chain go, and swinging round, under a lee shore, in eight fathoms of water, find ourselves lying out no more than a mile from land.

Then we drink tea; the pilgrims sing their evensong; and, with a thousand crossings and bendings, we commit our souls to heaven. Lying close in shore, under cover of a ridge of pines, we swing and lurch at our ease: but the storm howls angrily in our wake; and we know that many a poor crew, on their frail northern barks, are struggling all night with the powers of life and death. A Dutch clipper, called the "Ena," runs aground; her crew is saved and her cargo lost. Two Russian sloops are shattered and riven in our track; one of them parting amidships and going down in a trough of sea with every soul on board.

In the early watch the wind goes down; sunlight streaks the north-eastern sky; and, in the pink dawn, we catch, in our front, a little to the west, a glimpse of the green cupolas and golden crosses of Solovetsk—a joy and wonder to all eyes; not more to pilgrims who have walked a thousand miles to greet them, than they are to their English guest.

Saluting the holy place with prayer, and, steaming by a coast-line, broken by rocks and beautified by verdure, we pass, in a flood of soft warm sunshine, up a short inland reach, in which seals are plashing, over which doves are darting, each in their happy sport, and, by eight o'clock of a lovely August morning, swing ourselves round in a secluded bay under the Convent walls.

CHAPTER X.

The Holy Isles.

CHIEF in a group of rocks and banks lying off the Karel coast—a group not yet surveyed, and badly laid down in charts—Solovetsk is a small, green island, ten or twelve miles long, by eight or nine miles wide. The waters raging round her in this stormy sea have torn a way into the mass of stones and peat; forming many little coves and creeks; and near the middle, where the Convent stands, these waters have almost met. Hardly a mile of land divides the eastern bay from the western bay.

Solovetsk stands a little farther north than Vatna Jökull; the sixty-fifth degree of latitude passing close to the monastic pile. The rocks and islets lying round her are numerous and lovely, for the sea runs in and out among them, crisp with motion and light with foam; and their shores are everywhere green with mosses and fringed with forests of birch and pine. The lines are not tame, as on the Karel and Lapland coasts, for the ground swells upward into bluffs and downs, and one at least of these ridges may be called a hill. Each height is crowned by a white church, a green cupola, and a golden cross. On the down which may be called a hill stands a larger church, the belfry of which contains a light. Land, sea, and sky, are all in keeping; each a wonder and a beauty in the eyes of pilgrims of the stormy night.

Running alongside the wharf, on to which we step as easily as on to Dover Pier, we notice that beyond this beauty of nature, which man has done so much to point and gild, there is a bright and even a busy look about the commonest things. Groups of strange men dot the quays; Lopars, Karels, what not; but we soon perceive that Solovetsk is a civilised no less than an enchanted isle. The quay is spacious, the port is sweet and fresh. On our right lies that dock of which Father John was speaking with such pride. The "Hope," a more commodious pilgrim-boat than the "Faith," is lying on her stays. On our left stands a Guest House, looking so airy, light, and clean, that no hostelry on Italian lake could wear a more cheerful and inviting face. We notice a lift and crane; as things not seen in the trading ports; and one has hardly time to mark these signs of science ere noticing an iron tramway, running from the wharf to a great magazine of stores and goods.

A line of wall, with gates and towers, extends along the upper quay; and high above this line of wall, spring convent, palace, dome and cross. A stair leads up from the water to the Sacred Gates; and near the pathway from this stair we see two votive chapels; marking the spots on which the imperial pilgrims, Peter the Great and Alexander the Beneficent, landed from their boats.

Everything looks solid, many things look old.

Not to speak of the fortress walls and turrets, built of vast boulders, torn up from the sea-bed in the days of our own Queen Bess, the groups of palace, church, and belfry, rising within those walls, are of older date than any other work of man in this far-away corner of the globe. One cathedral—that of the Transfiguration—is older than the fortress walls. A second cathedral—that of the Ascension—dates from the time when St. Philip was Prior of Solovetsk. Besides having this air of antiquity, the place is alive with colour and instinct with a sense of art. The votive chapels which peep out here and there from among the trees are so many pictures; and these red crosses by the water-margin have been so arranged as to add a motive and a moral to the scene. Some broad, but not unsightly frescoes brighten the main front of the old cathedral, and similar pictures light the spandril of the Sacred Gates; while turrets and cupolas of church and chapel are everywhere gay with green and gold.

One dome, much noticed, and of rarest value in a Pilgrim's eye, is painted azure, fretted with golden stars. That dome is the crown of a new cathedral; built in commemoration of 1854—that Year of Wonders, when an English fleet was vanquished by the Mother of God. Within, the Convent looks more durable and splendid than without. Wall, rampart, guest-house, prison, tower, and church, are all of brick and stone. Every lobby is painted; often in a rude and early style; but these rough passages from Holy Writ have a sense and keeping higher than the morals conveyed by a coat of lime.

The screens and columns in the churches glow with a nobler art; though here, again, an eye, accustomed to admire no other than the highest of Italian work, will be only too ready to slight and scorn. The drawing is often weak, the pigment raw, the metal tawdry; yet these great breadths of gold and colour impress both eye and brain, especially when the lamps are lit, the psalm is raised, the incense burning, and the monks, attired in their long black hoods and robes, are ranged in front of the royal gates.

This pretty white house, under the Convent wall, near the Sacred Gates, was built in witness of a miracle, and is known as the Miracle Church. A pilgrim, eating a bit of white bread, which a pope had given him, let a crumb of it fall to the ground, when a strange dog tried to snatch it up. The crumb seemed to rise into the dog's mouth and then slip away from him, as though it were alive. That dog was the devil. Many persons saw this victory of the holy bread, and the monks of Solovetsk built a shrine on the spot to keep the memory of that miracle alive; and here it stands on the bay, between the chapels erected on the spots where Peter the Great and Alexander the Second landed from their ships.

When we come to drive, and sail, and walk into the recesses of this group of isles, we find them not less lovely than the first sweet promise of the bay in which we land. Forests surround, and lakelets pursue us, at every step. The wood is birch and pine; birch of the sort called silver, pine of the alpine stock. The trees are big enough for beauty, and the undergrowths are red with berries and bright with Arctic flowers. Here and there we come upon a clearing, with a dip into some green valley, in the bed of which slumbers a lovely lake. A scent of hay is in the air, and a perfume new to my nostrils, which my companions tell me breathes from the cotton-grass growing on the margin of every pool. At every turn of the road, we find a cross, well shaped and carved, and stained dark red; while the end of every forest lane is closed by a painted chapel, a lonely father's cell. A deep, soft silence reigns through earth and sky.

But the beauty of beauties lies in the lakes. More than a hundred of these lovely sheets of water nestle in the depths of pine-wood and birch-wood. Most famous of all these sheets is the Holy Lake, lying close behind the Convent wall; most beautiful of all, to my poor taste, is the White Lake, on the road to St. Savatie's cell and Striking Hill.

Holy Lake, a sheet of black water, deep and fresh, though it is not a hundred yards from the sea, has a function in the pilgrims' course. Arriving at Solovetsk, the bands of pilgrims march to this lake and strip to bathe. The waters are holy, and refresh the spirit while they purify the flesh. Without a word, the pilgrims enter a shed, throw off their rags, and leap into the flood; except some six or seven city-folk, who shiver in their shoes at the thought of that wholesome plunge. Their bath being finished, the pilgrims go to dinner and to prayers.

White Lake lies seven or eight miles from the Convent; sunk in a green hollow, with wooded banks, and a number of islets, stopping the lovely view with a yet more lovely pause. If St. Savatie had been an artist, one need not have wondered at his wandering into such a spot.

Yet the chief islet in this paradise of the Frozen Sea has one defect. When looking down from the belfry of Striking Hill on the intricate maze of sea and land, of lake and ridge, of copse and brake, of lawn and dell; each tender breadth of bright green grass, each sombre belt of dark-green pine, being marked by a white memorial church; you gaze and wonder, conscious of some hunger of the sense; it may be of the eye, it may be of the ear; your heart declaring all the while that, wealthy as the landscape seems, it lacks some last poetic charm. It is the want of animal life. No flock is in the meadow, and no herd is on the slope. No bark of dog comes on the air; no low of kine is on the lake. Neither cow nor calf, neither sheep nor lamb, neither goat nor kid, is seen in all the length of country from Striking Hill to the Convent gate. Man is here alone; and feels that he is alone.

This defect in the landscape is radical; not to be denied, and never to be cured. Not that cattle would not graze on these slopes and thrive in these woods. Three miles in front of Solovetsk stands the isle called Zaet, on which sheep and cattle browse; and five or six miles in the rear lies Moksalma, a large grassy isle, on which the poultry cackle, the horses feed, and the cows give milk. These animals would thrive on the holy isle, if they were not driven away by monastic rule; but Solovetsk has been sworn of the celibate order; and love is banished from the saintly soil. No mother is here permitted to fondle and protect her young; a great defect in landscapes otherwise lovely to eye and heart—a denial of nature in her tenderest forms.

The law is uniform, and kept with a rigour to which the imperial power itself must bend. No creature of the female sex may dwell on the isle. The peasants from the Karel coast are said to be so strongly impressed with the sin of breaking this rule, that they would rather leap into the sea than bring over a female cat. A woman may come in the pilgrim season to say her prayers, but that duty done, she must go her way. Summer is a time of license—a sort of carnival season, during which the letter of a golden rule is suspended for the good of souls. A woman may lodge in the Guest House, feed in the refectory; but she must quit the wards before nine at night. Some of the more holy chapels she may not enter; and her day of privilege is always short. A male pilgrim can reside at Solovetsk for a year; a female must be gone with the boats that bring her to the shrine. By an act of imperial grace, the commander of his Majesty's forces in the island,—an army some sixty strong,—is allowed to have his wife and children with him during the Pilgrims' year; that is to say, from June to August; but when the last boat returns to Archangel with the men of prayer, the lady and her little folk must leave their home in this holy place. A reign of piety and order is supposed to come with the early snows, and it is a question whether the Empress herself would be allowed to set her foot on the island in that better time.

The rule is easily enforced in the bay of Solovetsk, under the Convent walls; not so easily enforced at Zaet, Moksalma, and the still more distant isles, where tiny little convents have been built on spots inhabited by famous saints. In these more distant settlements it is hard to protect the holy men from female intrusion; for the Karel girls are fond of mischief, and they paddle about these isles in their light summer craft by day and night. The aged fathers only are allowed to live in such perilous spots.

CHAPTER XI.

The Local Saints.

THIS exclusion of women from the Holy Isle was the doing of Savatie, first of the Local Saints.

Savatie, the original anchoret of Solovetsk, was one day praying near a lake, when he heard a cry, as of a woman in pain. His comrade said it must have been a dream; for no woman was living nearer to their "desert" than the Karel coast. The saint went forth again to pray; but once again his devotions were disturbed by cries and sobs. Going round by the banks of the lake to see, he found a young woman lying on the ground, with her flesh all bruised, her back all bleeding, from recent blows. She was a fisherman's wife. On being asked who had done her this harm, she said that two young men, with bright faces and dressed in white raiment, came to her hut while her husband was away, and telling her she must go after him, as the land belonged to God, and no woman must sleep on it a single night, they threw her on the ground, struck her with rods, and made her cry with pain.

When she could walk, the poor creature got into her boat, and St. Savatie saw her no more. The fisherman came to fish, but his wife remained at home; and in this way woman was driven by angels from the Holy Isle. No monk, no layman, ever doubts this story. How can he? Here, to this day, stands the log-house in which Savatie dwelt, and twenty paces from it the mossy bank on which he knelt. Across the water there, beside yon clump of pines, rose the fisherman's shed. The sharp ascent, on which the church and lighthouse glisten, is still called Striking Hill.

This St. Savatie was a monk from Novgorod living at the old convent of Belozersk, in which he served the office of tonsurer—shaver of heads; but longing for a life of greater solitude than his convent gave him, he persuaded one of his brethren, named Valaam, to go up with him into the deserts near the Polar Sea. Boyars from his country-side were then going up into the north; and why should holy men not bear as much for Christ as boyars and traders bore for pelf? On praying all night in their chapels, these boyars and traders ran to their archbishop with the cry: "O give us leave, Vladika, to go forth, man and horse, and win new lands for St. Sophia." Settling in Kem, in Suma, in Soroka, and at other points, these men were adding a region larger than the mother country to the territories ruled by Novgorod the Great. The story of these boyars stirred up Savatie to follow in their wake, and labour in the desolate land which they were opening up.

Toiling through the virgin woods and sandy plains, Savatie and his companion Valaam arrived on the Vieg (in 1429), and found a pious monk, named German, who had also come from the South country. Looking towards the East, these monks perceived in the watery waste a group of isles; and trimming a light skiff, Savatie and German crossed the sea. Landing on the largest isle, they made a "desert" on the shore of a lakelet, lying at the foot of a hill on which birch and pine-trees grew to the top. Their lake was sheltered, the knoll was high; and from the summit they could see the sprinkle of isles and their embracing waves, as far as Orloff Cape to the south, the downs of Kem on the west.

Savatie brought with him a picture of the Virgin, not then known to possess miraculous virtues, which he hung up in a chapel built of logs. Near to this chapel he made for himself and his companion a hut of reeds and sticks, in which they lived in peace and prayer until the rigour of the climate wore them out. After six years spent in solitude, German sailed back to the Vieg; and Savatie, finding himself alone on the rock, in that Desert from which he had banished woman and love, became afraid of dying, without a priest being at hand to shrive and put him beneath the grass. Getting into his skiff, he also crossed to Soroka, where he obtained from Father Nathaniel, a Prior who had chanced to visit that town, the bread and cup; and then, his work on earth being done, he passed away to his eternal rest.

Laying him in the sands at Soroka, Nathaniel raised a chapel of pine-logs, dedicated to the Holy Trinity, above his grave; and there Savatie would have lain for ever, his name unknown, his saintly rank unrecognised, on earth, had he not fallen in the path of a man of stronger and more enduring spirit.

One of the bold adventurers from Novgorod, named Gabriel, settling with his wife Barbara, in the new village of Tolvui, on the banks of Lake Onega, had a son, whom he called Zosima, and devoted to God. Zosima, a monk while he was yet a child, took his vows in the monastery of Palaostrofsk, near his father's home; and on reaching the age when he could act for himself, he divided his inheritance among his kin, and taking up his pilgrim's staff departed for the north. At Suma he fell in with German, who told him of the life he had lived six years in his desert on the lonely rock. Zosima, taken by this tale, persuaded German to show him the spot where he and Savatie had dwelt so long. They crossed the sea. A lucky breeze bore them past Zaet, into a small and quiet bay; and when they leapt on shore—then strewn with boulders, and green with forest trees—they found themselves not only on the salt sea, but close to a deep and lustrous lake, the waters of which were sweet to the taste, and swarming with fish, the necessary food of monks.

Kneeling on the sand in prayer, Zosima was nerved by a miraculous Vision to found a religious colony in that lonely island, even as Marfa's people were founding secular colonies at Suma, Soroka, and Kem. He saw, as in a dream, a bright and comely monastic pile, with swelling domes and lofty turrets, standing on the brink of that lovely sheet of water—henceforth to be known as the Holy Lake. Starting from his knees, he told his companion, German, of the Vision he had seen;

described the walls, the Sacred Gates, the clusters of spires and domes; in a word, the Convent in the splendour of its present form. They cut down a pine, and framed it into a cross, which they planted in the ground; in token that this island in the frozen deep belonged to God and to His saints. This act of consecrating the isle took place (in 1436) a year after St. Savatie died.

The monks erected cabins near this cross; in which cabins they dwelt, about a mile apart, so as not to crowd upon each other in their desert home. The sites are marked by chapels erected to perpetuate their fame.

The tale of these young hermits living in their desert on the Frozen Sea being noised abroad in cloisters, monks from all sides of the north country came to join them; bringing strong thews and eager souls to aid in their task of raising up in that wild region, and among those savage tribes, a temple of the living God. In time a church grew round and above the original cross; and as none of the hermits were in holy orders, they sent a messenger to Yon, then Archbishop of Novgorod, asking him for a blessing on their work, and praying him to send them a Prior who could celebrate mass. Yon gave them his benediction and his servant Pavel. Pavel travelled into the north, and consecrated their humble church; but the climate was too hard for him to bear. A second Prior came out in Feodosie; a third Prior in Yon; both of whom stayed some time in the Frozen Sea, and only went back to

Novgorod when they were broken in health and advanced in years.

When Yon, the third Prior, left them, the Fathers held a meeting to consider their future course. Sixteen years had now passed by since Zosima and German crossed the sea from Suma; ten or twelve years since Pavel consecrated their humble church. In less than a dozen years three Priors had come and gone; and every one saw that monks who had grown old in the Volkhoff district, could not live in the Frozen Sea. The brethren asked their Archbishop to give them a Prior from their own more hardy ranks; and all these brethren joined in the prayer that Zosima, leader of the colony from first to last, would take this office of Prior upon himself. His poor opinion of himself gave place to a sense of the public good.

Marching on foot to Novgorod, a journey of more than a thousand miles, through a country without a road, Zosima went up to the great city, where he was received by the Vladika, and was ordained a priest. From the mayor and chief boyars, he obtained a more definite cession of the isles than Prior Yon had been able to secure; and thus he came back to his Convent as pope and Prior, with the fame of a holy man, to whom nothing might be denied. Getting leave to remove the bones of Savatie from Soroka to Solovetsk, he took up his body from the earth, and finding it pure and fresh, he laid the incorruptible relics in the crypt of his infant church.

More and more monks arrived in the lonely

isles; and pilgrims from far and near began to cross the sea; for the tomb of Savatie was said to work miraculous cures. But as the monastery grew in fame and wealth, the troubles of the world came down upon the Prior and his monks. The men of Kem began to see that this bank in the Frozen Sea was a valuable prize; and the lords of Anzersk and Moksalma quarrelled with the monks; disputing their right over the fore-shores, and pressing them with claims about the waifs and strays. At length, in his green old age, Zosima girded up his loins, and taking his pastoral staff in hand, set out for Novgorod, in the hope of seeing Marfa in person, and of settling, once and for ever, the question of his claim to these rocks by asking for the lordship of Kem itself to be vested in the Prior of Solovetsk!

On a column of the great Cathedral of St. Sophia, in the Kremlin of Novgorod, a series of frescoes tells the story of this visit of St. Zosima to the parent state. One picture takes the eye with a singular and abiding force—a banquet in a noble hall, in which the table is surrounded by headless guests.

Passing through the city from house to house, Zosima was received in nearly all with honour, as became his years and fame; but not in all. The boyars of Kem had friends in the city; and Marfa's ear had been filled with tales against his monkish guile and monkish greed. From her door he was driven with scorn; and her house was that in which he was most desirous of being received in peace.

Knowing that he could do nothing without her aid, Zosima set himself, by patient waiting on events, to overcome her fury against the cause which he was there to plead. At length, her feeling being subdued, she granted him a new charter (dated 1470, and still preserved at Solovetsk), confirming his right over all the lands, lakes, forests and foreshores of the Holy Isles, together with the lordship of Kem, made over, then and for all coming time, to the service of God.

Before Zosima left the great city, Marfa invited him to her table, where he was to take his leave, not only of herself, but of the chief boyars. As the Prior sat at meat, the company noticed that his face was sad, that his eyes were fixed on space, that his soul seemed moved by some unseen cause. "What is the matter?" cried the guests. He would not speak; and when they pressed around him closely, they perceived that burning drops were rolling down his cheeks. More eagerly than ever, they demanded to know what he saw in his fixed and terrible stare. "I see," said the monk, "six boyars at a feast, all seated at a table without their heads!"

That dinner-party is the subject painted on the column in St. Sophia; and the legend says that every man who sat with him that day at Marfa's table had his head sliced off by Ivan the Third, when the proud and ancient republic fell before the destroyer of the Golden Horde.

Strengthened by his new titles, Zosima came back to Solovetsk a prince; and the pile which he governed took the style, which it has ever since borne, of

The Convent that Endureth for Ever.

Zosima ruled his Convent as Prior for twenty-six years; and after a hermitage of forty-two years on his lowly rock he passed away into his rest.

On his dying couch he told his disciples that he was about to quit them in the flesh, but only in the flesh. He promised to be with them in the spirit; watching in the same cells, and kneeling at the same graves. He bade them thank God daily for the promise that their Convent should endure for ever; safe as a rock, and sacred as a shrine—even though it stood in the centre of a raging sea—in the reach of pitiless foes. And then he passed away—the second of these local saints—leaving, as his legacy to mankind, the temporal and spiritual germs of this great sanctuary in the Frozen Sea.

About that time, the third monk also died. German, the companion of Savatie, in his cabin near Striking Hill; afterwards of Zosima, in his hut by the Holy Lake. He died at Novgorod, to which city he had again returned from the north. His bones were begged from the monks, in whose grounds they lay, and being carried to Solovetsk, were laid in a shrine near the graves of his ancient and more famous friends.

Such was the origin of the Convent, over which the Archimandrite Feofan now rules and reigns.

CHAPTER XII.

A Monastic Household.

My letter from his Sanctity of Archangel having been sent in to Feofan, Archimandrite of Solovetsk, an invitation to the palace arrives in due form by the mouth of Father Hilarion; who may be described to the lay world as the Archimandrite's minister for secular affairs. Father Hilarion is attended by Father John, who seems to have taken upon himself the office of my companion-in-chief. Attiring myself in befitting robes, we pass through the Sacred Gates, and after pausing for a moment to glance at the models of Peter's yacht and frigate, there laid up, and to notice some ancient frescoes which line the passage, we mount a flight of steps, and find ourselves standing at the Archimandrite's door.

The chief of this monastery is a great man; one of the greatest men in the Russian church; higher, as some folks say, than many a man who calls himself bishop, and even metropolite. Since the days of Peter the Great, the monastery of Solovetsk has been an independent spiritual power; owning no master in the Church, and answering to no authority save that of the Holy Governing Synod.

Like an archbishop, the Archimandrite of Solovetsk has the right to bless his congregation by waving three tapers in his right hand over two tapers in his left. He lives in a palace; he receives four thousand rubles a-year in money; and the cost of his house, his table, his vestments, and his boats, comes out of the monastic fund. He has a garden, a vineyard, and a country-house; and his choice of a cell in the sunniest nooks of these sacred isles. His personal rank is that of a prince, with a dignity which no secular rank can give; since he reigns alike over the bodies and the souls of men.

Dressed in his cowl and frock, on which hangs a splendid sapphire cross, Feofan, a small, slight man—with the ascetic face, the womanlike curls, and vanishing figure, which you note in nearly all these celibate priests—advances to meet us near the door, and after blessing Father John, and shaking me by the hand, he leads us to an inner room, hung with choice prints, and warmed by carpets and rugs, where he places me on the sofa by his side, while the two fathers stand apart, in respectful attitude, as though they were in church.

"You are not English?" he inquires, in a tender tone, just marked by a touch—a very light touch —of humour.

"Yes, English certainly."

A turn of his eye, made slowly, and by design, directs my attention to his finger, which reclines on an object hardly to have been expected on an Archimandrite's table; an iron shell! The Tower mark proves that it must have been fired from an English gun. A faint smile flits across the Archimandrite's face. There it stands; an English shell, unburst; the stopper drawn; and two plugs near it on a tray. That missile, it is clear, must have fallen into some soft bed of sand or peat.

"You are the first Pilgrim who ever came from your country to Solovetsk," says Feofan, smiling. "One man came before you in a steamship; he was an engineer—one Anderson; you know him, maybe? No! He was a good man—he minded his engines well; but he could not live on fish and quass—he asked for beef and beer; and when we told him we had none to give him, he went away. No other English ever came."

He passes on to talk of the Holy Sepulchre and the Russian convent near the Jaffa Gate.

"You are welcome to Solovetsk," he says at parting; "see what you wish to see, go where you wish to go, and come to me when you like." Nothing could be sweeter than his voice, nothing softer than his smile, as he spake these words; and seeing the twinkle in his eye, as we stand near the English shell, I also smile and add: "On the mantel-piece of my writing-room in London there lies just such another shell, a trifle thinner in the girth."

"Yes?" he asks, a little curious—for a monk.

"My shell has the Russian mark; it was fired from Sevastopol, and picked up by a friend of my own in his trench before the Russian lines."

Feofan laughs, so far as an Archimandrite ever laughs—in the eyes and about the mouth. From this hour his house and household are at my disposal—his boat, his carriage, and his driver; everything is done to make my residence in the Convent pleasant; and every night my host is good enough to receive from his officers a full report of what I have seen and what I have said during the day!

Three hundred monks of all classes reside on the Holy Isle. The chief is, of course, the Archimandrite; next to him come forty monks, who are also popes; then come seventy or eighty monks who wear the hood and have taken the final vows; after these orders come the postulants, acolytes, singers, servants. Lodgers, scholars, and hired laymen fall into a second class.

These brethren are of all ages and conditions, from the pretty child who serves at table to the decrepid father who cannot leave his cell; from the monk of noble birth and ample fortune to the brother who landed on these islands as a tramp. They wear the same habit, eat at the same board, listen to the same chants, and live the same life. Each brother has his separate cell, in which he sleeps and works; but every one, unless infirm with years and sickness, must appear in chapel at the hour of prayer, in refectory at the hour of meals. Hood and gown, made of the same serge, and cut in the same style, must be worn by all, excepting only by the priest who reads the service for the day. They suffer their beards and locks to grow, and spend much time in combing and smoothing these abundant growths. A flowing beard is the pride of monks and men; but while the beard is coming, a young fellow combs and parts his hair with all the coquetry of a girl. When looking at a bevy of boys in a church, their heads uncovered, their locks, shed down the centre, hanging about their shoulders, you might easily mistake them for singers of the sweeter sex.

Not many of these fathers could be truly described as ordinary men. A few are pure fanatics, who fear to lose their souls; still more are men with a natural calling for religious life. A goodly list are prisoners of the church, sent up from convents in the south and west. These last are the salt and wine of Solovetsk; the men who keep it sweet and make it strong. The offence for which they suffer is too much zeal:—a learned and critical spirit, a disposition to find fault, a craving for reform, a wish to fall back on the purity of ancient times. For such disorders of the mind an ordinary monk has no compassion; and a journey to the desert of Solovetsk is thought to be for such diseases the only cure.

An Archimandrite, appointed to his office by the Holy Governing Synod, must be a man of learning and ability, able to instruct his brethren and to rule his house. He is expected to burn like a shining light, to fast very often, to pray very much, to rise very early, and to live like a saint. The brethren keep an eye upon their chief. If he is hard with himself he may be hard with them; but woe to him if he is weak in the flesh—if he wears fine linen about his throat, if savoury dishes steam upon his board, if the riumka—that tiny glass out of which whisky is drunk—goes often to his lips.

'In every monk about his chamber he finds a critic; in nearly every one he fears a spy. It is not easy to satisfy them all. One father wishes for a sterner life, another thinks the discipline too strict. By every post some letters of complaint go out, and every member of the Holy Governing Synod may be told in secret of the Archimandrite's sins. If he fails to win his critics, the appeals against his rule increase in number and in boldness, till at length inquiry is begun, bad feeling is provoked on every side, and the offending chieftain is promoted—for the sake of peace—to some other place.

The Archimandrite of Solovetsk has the assistance of three great officers, who may be called his manager, his treasurer, and his custodian; officers who must be not only monks but popes.

Father Hilarion is the manager, with the duty of conducting the more worldly business of his Convent. It is he who lodges the guests when they arrive, who looks after the ships and docks, who employs the labourers and conducts the farms, who sends out smacks to fish, who deals with skippers, who buys and sells stores, who keeps the workshops in order, and who regulates the coming and going of the Pilgrims' boat. It is he who keeps church and tomb in repair, who sees that the fathers are warmly clad, who takes charge of the buildings and furniture, who superintends the kitchen, who keeps an eye on corridor and yard, who orders books and prints, who manages the painting-room and the photographer's office, who inspects the cells, and provides that every one has a bench, a press, a looking-glass, and a comb.

Father Michael is the treasurer, with the duty of receiving all gifts and paying all accounts. The income of the monastery is derived from two sources; from the sale of what is made in the monkish workshops; and from the gifts of pilgrims and of those who send offerings by pilgrims. No one can learn how much they receive from either source; for the receiving-boxes are placed in corners, and the contributor is encouraged to conceal from his left hand what his right hand drops in. Forty thousand rubles a-year has been mentioned to me as the sum received in gifts; but five thousand pounds must be far below the amount of money passing in a year under Father Michael's eye. It is probably eight or ten. The charities of these monks are bounded only by the power of the people to come near them; and in the harder class of winters the peasants and fishermen push through the floes of ice from beyond Orloff Cape and Kandalax Bay in search of a basket of Convent bread. These folks are always fed when they arrive, are always supplied with loaves when they depart. The schools, too, cost no little; for the monks receive all boys who come to them—sent, as they hold, by the Father whom they serve.

Father Alexander is the custodian, with the duty of keeping the monastic wardrobe, together with the ritual books, the charters and papers, the jewels and the altar plate. His office is in the sacristy, with the treasures of which he is perfectly familiar, from the letter, in Cyrilian character and Slavonic phrase, by which Marfa of Novgorod gave this islet to the monks, down to that pious reliquary in which are kept some fragments of English shells; kept with as much veneration as bones of saints and chips from the genuine cross!

CHAPTER XIII.

A Pilgrim's Day.

A PILGRIM'S day begins in the early morning, and lengthens late into the night.

At two o'clock, when it has hardly yet grown dark in our cells, a monk comes down the passage, tinkling his bell and droning out, "Rise and come to prayer." Starting at his cry, we huddle on our clothes, and rush from our hot rooms, heated by stoves, into the open air; men and women, boys and girls, boatmen and woodmen, hurrying through the night towards the Sacred Gates.

At half-past two the first matins commence in the new church—the Miracle Church—dedicated to the Victress, Mother of God; in which lie the bones of St. Savatie and St. Zosima, in the corner, as the highest place. A hundred lamps are lit, and the wall-screen of pictured saints glows richly in our sleepy eyes. Men and women, soldiers and peasants, turn into that sacred corner where the saints repose, cross themselves sevèn times, bow their foreheads to the ground, and kiss the pavement before the shrine.

Falling into our places near the altar-screen; arranging ourselves in files, rank behind rank, in open order, so that each can kneel and kiss the ground without pushing against his neighbour; we stand erect, uncovered, while the pope recites his office, and the monks respond their chant. These matins are not over until four o'clock.

A second service opens in the old Cathedral at half-past three, and lasts until half-past five; and when the first pope has given his blessing, some of the more ardent Pilgrims rush from the Virgin's church to the Cathedral, where they stand in prayer, and kneel to kiss the stones for ninety minutes more; at the end of which time they receive a second benediction from a second pope.

An hour is now spent by the Pilgrims in either praying at the tombs of saints, or pacing a long gallery, so contrived as to connect the several churches and other monastic buildings by a covered way. Along the walls of this gallery rude and early Russian artists have painted the joys of heaven, the pains of purgatory, and the pangs of hell. These pictures seize the eyes of my fellow-pilgrims, though in quaint and dramatic terror they sink below the level of such old work in the Gothic cloisters of the Rhine. A Russian painter has no variety of invention; a devil is to him a monkey with a spiked tail and a tongue of flame; and hell itself is only a hot place in which sinners are either fried by a fiend, or chawed up, flesh and bone, by a monstrous bear. Yet, children sometimes swoon, and women go mad from fright, on seeing these threats of a future state. My own poor time is given to scanning a miraculous picture of Jerusalem, said to have been painted on the staircase by a monk of Solovetsk, as a Vision of the Holy City, seen by him in a dream.

After studying the details for a while, I recognise in this Vision of the holy man a plan of Olivet and Zion copied from an old Greek print!

All this time the Pilgrims are bound to fast.

At seven o'clock the bells announce early mass, and we repair to the Miracle Church, where, after due crossings and prostration before the tomb, we fall into rank as before, and listen for an hour and a half to the sacred ritual, chanted with increasing fire.

When this first mass is over, the time being nearly nine o'clock, the weaker brethren may indulge themselves with a cup of tea; but the better Pilgrim denies himself this solace, as a temptation of the Evil Spirit; and even his weaker brother has not much time to dally with the fumes of his darling herb. The great bell in the convent-yard, a gift of the reigning Emperor, and one more witness to the Year of Wonders, warns us that the highest service of the day is close at hand.

Precisely at nine o'clock the monks assemble in the cathedral to celebrate high mass; and the congregation being already met, the tapers are lit, the deacon begins to read, the clergy take up the responses, and the officiating priest, arrayed in his shining cope and cap, recites the old and mystical forms of Slavonic prayer and praise. Two hours by the clock we stand in front of that golden shrine; stand on the granite pavement—all uncovered, many unshod—listening with ravished ears to what is certainly the noblest ceremonial music of the Russian Church.

High mass being sung and said, we ebb back slowly from the cathedral into the long gallery, where we have a few minutes more of purgatorial fire, and then a monk announces dinner, and the devoutest Pilgrim in the band accepts his signal with a thankful look.

The dining-hall to which we adjourn with some irregular haste is a vaulted chamber below the cathedral, and in any other country than Russia would be called a crypt. But men must build according to their clime. The same church would not serve for winter and summer, on account of the cold and heat; and hence a sacred edifice is nearly always divided into an upper and a lower church; the upper tier being used in summer, the lower tier in winter. Our dining-hall at Solovetsk is the winter church.

Long tables run down the room, and curl round the circular shaft, which sustains the cathedral floor. On these tables the first course is already laid; a tin plate for each guest, in which lie a wooden spoon, a knife and fork; and by the side of this tin platter a pound of rye-bread. The Pilgrims are expected to dine in messes of four, like monks. A small tin dish is laid between each mess, containing one salted sprat, divided into four bits by a knife, and four small slices of raw onion. To each mess is given a copper tureen of sour quass, and a dish of salt cod-fish, broken into small lumps, boiled down, and left to cool.

A bell rings briskly; up we start, cross ourselves seven times, bow towards the floor, sit down again,

The captain of each mess throws pepper and salt into the dish, and stirs up our pottage with the ladle out of which he drinks his quass. A second bell rings; we dip our wooden ladles into the dish of cod. A reader climbs into the desk, and drawls the story of some saint, while a youth carries round a basket of white bread, already blessed by the priest and broken into bits. Each Pilgrim takes his piece and eats it, crossing himself, time after time, until the morsel gets completely down his throat.

A third bell rings. Hush of silence; sound of prayer. Serving-men appear; our platters are swept away; a second course is served. The boys who wait on us, with rosy cheeks, smooth chins, and hanging locks, look very much like girls. This second course, consisting of a tureen of cabbage-soup, takes no long time to eat. A new reader mounts the desk, and gives us a little more life of saint. A fourth bell jangles; much more crossing takes place; the serving-men rush in; our tables are again swept clean.

Another course is served; a soup of fresh herrings, caught in the Convent bay; the fish very good and sweet. Another reader; still more life of saint; and then a fifth bell rings.

A fourth and last course now comes in; a dainty of barley paste, boiled rather soft, and eaten with sour milk. Another reader; still more life of saint; and then sixth bell. The Pilgrims rise; the reader stops, not caring to finish his story; and our meal is done.

Our meal, but not the ritual of that meal. Rising

from our bench, we fall once more into rank and file; the women, who have dined in a room apart, crowd back into the crypt; and we join our voices in a sacred song. Then we stand for a little while in silence, each with his head bent down, as humbling ourselves before the screen, during which a pope distributes to each pilgrim a second morsel of consecrated bread. Brisk bell rings again; the monks raise a psalm of thanksgiving; a pope pronounces the benediction; and then the diners go their way refreshed with the bread and fish.

It is now near twelve o'clock. The next church service will not be held until a quarter to four in the afternoon. In the interval we have the long cloister to walk in; the holy lake to see; the shrine of St. Philip to inspect; the tombs of good monks to visit; the priestly robes and monastic jewels to admire; with other distractions to devour the time. We go off, each his own way; some into the country, which is full of tombs and shrines of the lesser saints; others to lave their limbs in the holy lake; not a few to the cells of monks who vend crosses, amulets, and charms. A Russian is a believer in stones, in rings, in rosaries, in rods; for he bears about him a hundred relics of his ancient pagan creeds. His favourite amulet is a cross, which he can buy in brass for a kopek; one form for a man, a second form for a woman; the masculine form being Nikon's cross, with a true Greek cross in relief; the feminine form being a mixture of the two. Once tied round the neck, this amulet is never to be taken off, on peril of sickness and sudden death.

To drop it is a fault, to lose it is a sin. A second talisman is a bone ball, big as a pea, hollow, drilled and fitted with a screw. A drop of mercury is coaxed into the hole, and the screw being turned, the charm is perfect, and the ball is fastened to the cross. This talisman protects the wearer from contagion in the public baths.

Some Pilgrims go in boats to the farther isles; to Zaet, where two aged monks reside, and a flock of sheep browses on the herbage; to Moksalma, a yet more secular spot, where the cattle feed, and the poultry cluck and crow, in spite of St. Savatie's rule. These islets supply the Convent with milk and eggs, in which holy men rejoice as a relief from fish, in nature's own old-fashioned ways.

Not a few of the Pilgrims, finding that a special pope has been appointed to show things to their English guest, perceive that the way to see sights is to follow that pope. They have to be told—in a kindly voice—that they are not to follow him into the Archimandrite's room. To-day, they march in his train into the wardrobe of the Convent, where the copes, crowns, staffs and crosses employed in these church services are kept; a rich and costly collection of robes, embroided with flowers and gold, and sparkling with rubies, diamonds, and pearls. Many of these robes are gifts of emperors and tsars. One of the costliest is the gift of Ivan the Terrible; but even this splendid garment pales before a gift of Alexander, the reigning prince, who sent the Archimandrite—in remembrance of the

Virgin's victory—a full set of canonicals, from crown and staff to robe and shoe.

Exactly at a quarter before four o'clock, a bell commands us to return; for vespers are commencing in the Miracle church. Again, we kneel at the tombs and kiss the stones, the hangings, and the iron rails; after which we fall in as before, and listen while the vespers are intoned by monks and boys. This service concludes at half-past four. Adjourning to the long gallery, we have another look at the fires of purgatory and the abodes of bliss. Five minutes before six, we file into the Cathedral for second vespers, and remain there standing and uncovered—some of us unshod—until half-past seven.

At eight, the supper bell rings. Our company gathers at the welcome sound; the monks form a procession; the Pilgrims trail on; all moving with a hungry solemnity to the crypt, where we find the long tables groaning, as at dinner, with the pound of black bread, the salt sprat, the onion parted into four small pieces with a knife, and the copper tureen of quass. Our supper is the dinner served up afresh, with the same prayers, the same bowing and crossing, the same bell-ringing, and the same life of saint. The only difference is, that in the evening we have no barley-paste and no stale milk.

When every one is filled and the fragments are picked up, we rise to our feet; recite a thanksgiving, and join the Fathers in their evening song. A pope pronounces a blessing, and then we are free to go into our cells.

A Pilgrim who can read, and may happen to

have good books about him, is expected, on retiring to his cell, to read through a Psalm of David, and to ponder a little on the Lives of Saints. The Convent gates are closed at nine o'clock; when it is thought well for the Pilgrim to be in bed.

At two in the morning, a monk will come into his lobby, tinkle the bell, and call him to the duties of another day.

CHAPTER XIV.

Prayer and Labour.

BUT if the hours given up to prayer at Solovetsk are many, the hours given up to toil are more. This Convent is a hive of industry, not less remarkable for what it does in the way of work than for what it is in the way of art and prayer.

"Pray and work" was the maxim of monastic houses, when monastic houses had a mission in the West. "Pray and work," said Peter the Great to his council. But such a maxim is not in harmony with the existing system; not in harmony with the Byzantine church; and what you find at Solovetsk is traceable to an older and a better source. No monk in this sanctuary leads an idle life. Not only the fathers who are not yet popes, but many of those who hold the staff and give the benediction, devote their talents to the production of things which may be useful in the church, in the refectory, and in the cell. A few make articles for sale in the outer world; such articles as bread, clothes, rosaries, and spoons. All round these ramparts, within the walls, you find a row of workshops, in which there is a hum of labour from early dawn until long after dark; forges, dairies, salting-rooms, studies, ship-yards, bake-houses, weaving-sheds, rope-walks, sewing-rooms, fruit-stores, breweries, boot-stalls, and the like, through all the forms which industry takes in a civilised age. These monks appear to be masters of every craft. They make nearly everything you can name, from beads to frigates; and they turn out everything they touch in admirable style. No whiter bread is baked, no sweeter quass is brewed, than you can buy in Solovetsk. To go with Father Hilarion on his round of inspection is to meet a dozen surprises face to face. At first the whole exhibition is like a dream; and you can hardly fancy that such things are being done by a body of monks, in a lonely islet, locked up from the world for eight months in the twelve by storms of sleet and deserts of ice.

These monks make seal-skin caps and belts; they paint in oil and carve in wood; they cure and tan leather; they knit woollen hose; they cast shafts of iron; they wind and spin thread; they polish stones; they cut out shoes and felts; they mould pewter plates; they dry fruit; they fell and trim forest trees; they clip paper flowers; they build carts and sledges; they embroider capes and bands; they bake bricks; they weave baskets and panniers of silver bark; they quarry and hew blocks of stone; they paint soup-ladles; they design altar-pieces, chapels, and convents; they refine bees'-wax; they twist cord and rope; they forge anchors and marling-spikes; they knit and sew, and ply their needles in every branch of useful and decorative art. In all these departments of industry, the thing which they turn out is an example of honest work.

Many of the fathers find a field for their talents on the farm; in breeding cattle, in growing potatoes, in cutting grass, in shearing sheep, in rearing poultry, in churning butter and making cheese. A few prefer the more poetic labour of the garden; pruning grapes, bedding strawberries, hiving bees, and preserving fruit. The honey made at Mount Alexander is pure and good, the wax is also white and fine.

The Convent bakehouse is a thing to see. Boats run over from every village on the coast to buy Convent bread; often to beg it; and every Pilgrim who comes to pray takes with him one loaf as a parting gift. This Convent bread is of two sorts—black and white—leavened and unleavened—domestic and consecrated. The first is cheap, and eaten at every meal; the second is dear, and eaten as an act of grace. Both kinds are good. A consecrated loaf is small, weighing six or eight ounces, and is stamped with a sacred sign and blessed by a pope. The stamp is a cross, with a legend running round the border in old Slavonic type. These small white loaves of unleavened bread are highly prized by pious people; and a man who visits such a monastery as either Solovetsk, St. George, or Troitsa, cannot bring back to his servants a gift more precious in their eyes than a small white loaf.

The brewery is no less perfect in its line than the bakehouse. Quass is the Russian ale and beer in one; the national drink; consumed by all classes, mixed with nearly every dish. Solovetsk has a name and fame for this Russian brew.

Connected with these good things of the table

are the workshops for carving platters and painting spoons. The arts of life are simple in these northern wilds; forks are seldom seen; and knives are not much used. The instrument by which a man mostly helps himself to his dinner is a spoon. Nearly all his food is boiled; his cabbage-soup, his barley mess, his hash of salt-cod, his dish of sour milk. A deep platter lies in the centre of his table, and his homely guests sit round it, armed with their capacious spoons. Platter and spoon are carved of wood, and sometimes they are painted with skill and taste; though the better sorts are kept by Pilgrims rather as keepsakes than for actual use.

A branch of industry allied to carving spoons and platters, is that of twisting baskets and panniers into shape. Crockery in the forest is rude and dear, and in a long land journey the weight of three or four pots and cups would be a serious strain. From bark of trees they weave a set of baskets for personal and domestic use, which are lighter than cork and handier than tin. You close them by a lid, and carry them by a loop. They are perfectly dry and sweet; with just a flavour, but no more, of the delicious resin of the tree. They hold milk. You buy them of all sizes, from that of a pepper-box to that of a water-jar; obtaining a dozen for a few kopeks.

The panniers are bigger and less delicate, made for rough passage over stony roads and through bogs of mire. These panniers are fitted with compartments, like a vintner's crate, in which you can stow away bottles of wine and insinuate knives and forks. In the open part of your pannier it is well (if you are packing for a long drive) to have an assortment of bark baskets, in which to carry such trifles as mustard, cream, and salt.

Among the odds and ends of workshops into which you drop, is that of the weaving-shed, in one of the turrets on the Convent wall; a turret which is noticeable not only for the good work done in the looms, but for the part which it had to play in the defence of Solovetsk against the English fleet. The shot which is said to have driven off the "Brisk" was fired from this Weaver's tower.

Peering above a sunny corner of the rampart stands the photographic chamber; and near to this chamber, in a new range of buildings, are the cells in which the painters and enamellers toil. The sun makes pictures of anything in his range; boats, islets, pilgrims, monks; but the artists toiling in these cells are all employed in devotional art. Some are only copiers; and the most expert are artists only in a conventional sense. This country is not yet rich in art, except in that hard Byzantine style which Nikon the Patriarch allowed in private houses, and enforced in Convent, Shrine, and Church.

But these Fathers pride themselves, not without cause, on being greater in their works by sea than even in their works by land. Many of them live on board, and take to the water as to their mothers' milk. They are rich in boats, in rigging, and in nets. They wind excellent rope and cord. They know how to light and buoy dangerous points and armlets. They keep their own lighthouses. They build lorchas and sloops; and they have found by trial that a steamship can be turned off the stocks at Solovetsk, of which every part, from the smallest brass nail to the main-mast (with the sole exception of her engines), is the produce of their toil.

That vessel is called the "Hope." Her crew is mainly a crew of monks; and her captain is not only a monk—like Father John—but an actual pope. My first sight of this priestly skipper is in front of the royal gates where he is celebrating mass.

This reverend Father takes me after service to see his vessel and the dock in which she lies. Home-built and rigged, the "Hope" has charms in my eyes possessed by very few ships. A steamer made by monks in the Frozen Sea, is in her way as high a feat of mind as the spire of Notre Dame in Antwerp, as the cathedral front at Wells. The thought of building that steamer was conceived in a monkish brain; the lines were fashioned by a monkish pen; monks felled the trees, and forged the bolts, and wove the canvas, and curled the ropes. Monks put her together; monks painted her cabin; monks stuffed her seats and pillows. Monks launched her on the sea, and, since they have launched her, they have sailed in her from port to port.

"How did you learn your trade of skipper?"

The Father smiles. He is a young fellow—younger than Father John; a fellow of thirty or thirty-two, with swarthy cheek, black eye, and tawny mane; a man to play the pirate in some drama of virtuous love. "I was a seaman in my youth," he says; "and when we wanted a skipper in the Convent, I went over to Kem, where we have a school of navigation, and got the certificate of a master; that entitled me to command my ship."

"The council of that school are not very strict?"

"No; not with monks. We have our own ways; we labour in the Lord; and He protects us in what we do for Him."

"Through human means?"

"No; by His own right hand, put forth under all men's eyes. You see, the first time that we left the Convent for Archangel, we were weak in hands and strange to our work. A storm came on; the 'Hope' was driven on shore. Another crew would have taken to their boats and lost their ship, if not their lives. We prayed to the Most Pure Mother of God; at first she would not hear us on account of our sins; but we would not be denied, and sang our psalms until the wind went down."

"You were still ashore?"

"Yes; grooved in a bed of sand; but when the wind veered round, the ship began to heave and stir. We tackled her with ropes and got her afloat once more. Slava Bogu! It was Her act!"

The dock of which Father John spoke with pride turns out to be not a dock only, but a dry dock! Now, a dock, even where it is a common dock, is one of those signs by which one may guage—as by the strength of a city wall, the splendour of a court of justice, and the beauty of a public garden,—the height to which a people have attained. In Russia docks are extremely rare. Not a dozen ports in the empire can boast a dock. Archangel has no dock;

Astrachan has no dock; Rostoff has no dock. It is only in such cities as Riga and Odessa, built and occupied by foreigners, that you find such things. The dry dock at Solovetsk is the only sample of its kind in the whole of Russia Proper! Cronstadt has a dry dock; but Cronstadt is in Finnish waters—a German port, with a German name. The only work of this kind existing on Russian ground is the product of monkish enterprise and skill.

Priests take their share in all these labours. When a monk enters into orders he is free to devote himself, if he chooses, to the Church service only, since the Holy Governing Synod recognises the right of a pope to a maintenance in his office; but in the Convent of Solovetsk, a priest rarely confines his activity to his sacred duties. Work is the sign of a religious life. If any man shows a talent for either art or business, he is excited by the praise of his fellows and superiors to pursue the call of his genius, devoting the produce of his labour to the glory of God. One pope is a farmer, a second a painter, a third a fisherman; this man is a collector of simples, that a copier of manuscripts, and this again, a binder of books.

Of these vocations that of the schoolmaster is not the least coveted. All children who come to Solovetsk are kept for a year, if not for a longer time. The lodging is homely and the teaching rough; for the schools are adapted to the state of the country; and the food and sleeping-rooms are raised only a little above the comforts of a peasant's home. No one is sent away untaught; but only a few are kept beyond a year. If a lad likes to remain and work in the Convent he can hire himself out as a labourer, either in the fishing-boats or on the farms. He dines in summer, like the monks, on bread, fish, and quass; in winter he is provided with salt mutton, cured on the farm—a luxury his masters may not touch. Many of these boys remain for life, living in a celibate state, like the monks; but sure of a dinner and a bed, safe from the conscription, and free from family cares. Some of them take vows. If they go back into the world they are likely to find places on account of their past; in any case, they can shift for themselves, since a lad who has lived a few years in this Convent is pretty sure to be able to fish and farm, to cook his own dinner, and to mend his own boots.

CHAPTER XV.

Black Clergy.

ALL men of the higher classes in Russia talk of their Black Clergy as a body of worthless fellows; idle, ignorant, profligate; set apart by their vows as unsocial; to whom no terms should be offered, with whom no capitulations need be kept. "Away with them, root and branch!" is a general cry, delivered by young and liberal Russians in the undertone of a fixed resolve.

The men who raise this cry are not simply scoffers and scorners, making war on religious ideas and ecclesiastical institutions. Only too often they are men who love their church, who support their parish priests, and who wish to plant their country in the foremost line of Christian states. Russia, they say, possesses ten thousand monks; and these ten thousand monks they would hand over to a drill serjeant and convert into regiments of the line.

This rancour of the educated classes towards the monks—a rancour roused and fed by their undying hatred of reforms in church and state—compels one to mark the extent and study the sources of monastic power. This study will take us far and wide; though it will also bring us in the end to Solovetsk once more.

"A desert dotted with cloisters," would be no

untrue description of the country spreading southward from the Polar Sea to the Tartar Steppe. In New Russia, in the khanates of Kazan and Crimea, in the steppes of the Lower Volga, and in the wastes of Siberia, it would not be true. But Great Russia is a paradise of monks. In the vast regions stretching from Kem to Belgorod—an eagle's flight from north to south of a thousand miles—from Pskoff on Lake Peipus, to Vasil on the Middle Volga—a similar flight from west to east of seven hundred miles—the land is everywhere bright with cloisters, musical with monastic bells.

Nothing on this earth's surface can be drearier than a Russian forest, unless it be a Russian plain. The forest is a growth of stunted birch and pine; the trees of one height and girth; the fringe of black shoots unvaried save by some break of bog, some length of colourless lake. The plain is a stretch of moor, without a swell, without a tree, without a town, for perhaps a hundred leagues; on which the grass, if grass such herbage can be called, is brown; while the village, if such a scatter of cabins can be called by a name so tender and picturesque, is nothing but log and mud. A traveller's eye would weary, and his heart would sicken, at the long succession of such lines, were it not that here and there, in the opening of some forest glade, on the ridge of some formless plain, the radiant cross and sparkling towers of a convent spring towards heaven; a convent with its fringe of verdure, its white front, its clustering domes and chains. The woods round Kargopol, the marshes near Lake

Ilmen, and the plains of Moscow, are alive with light and colour; while the smaller convents on river bank and in misty wood, being railed and painted, look like works of art. One of my sweetest recollections in a long, dull journey, is that of our descent into the valley of Siya, when we sighted the great monastery, lying in a watery dell amidst groves of trees, with the rays of a setting sun on her golden cross and her shining domes—a happy valley and a consecrated home; not to speak of such trifles as the clean cell and the wholesome bread which a Pilgrim finds within her walls!

The old cities of Great Russia—Novgorod, Moscow, Pskoff, Vladimir—are much richer in monastic institutions than their rivals of a later time. For leagues above and leagues below the ancient capital of Russia, the river Volkhoff, on the banks of which it stands, is bright with these old mansions of the church. Novgorod enriched her suburbs with the splendid convents of St. George, St. Cyril, and of St. Anton of Rome. Moscow lies swathed in a belt and mantle of monastic houses—Simonoff, Donskoi, Danieloff, Alexiefski, Ivanofski, and many more; the belfries and domes of which lighten the wonderful panorama seen from the Sparrow Hills. Pskoff has her glorious convent of the Catacombs, all but rivalling that of Kief.

Within the walls, these cloisters are no less splendid than the promise from without. Their altars and chapels are always fine, the refectories neat and roomy, the sacristies rich in crosses and priestly robes. Many fine pictures—fine of their school—

adorn the screens and the royal gates. Nearly all possess portraits of the Mother and Child encased in gold, and some have lamps and croziers worth their weight in sterling coin. The greater part of what is visible of Russian wealth appears to hang around these shrines.

These old monastic houses sprang out of the social life around them. They were centres of learning, industry, and art. A convent was a school, and in these schools a special excellence was sought and won. This stamp has never been effaced; and many of the convents still aspire to excellence in some special craft. The Convent of St. Sergie, near Strelna, is famed for music; the New Monastery, near Kherson, for melons; the Troitsa, near Moscow, for carving; the Catacombs, near Kief, for service-books.

In the belfry of the old cathedral of St. Sophia at Novgorod you are shown a chamber which was formerly used as a treasure-room by the citizens—in fact, as their place of safety and their tower of strength. You enter it through a series of dark and difficult passages, barred by no less than twelve iron doors; each door to be unfastened by bolt and bar, secured in the catches under separate lock and key. In this strong place the burghers kept, in times of peril, their silver plate, their costly icons, and their ropes of pearl. A robber would not—and a boyar dared not—force the sanctuary of God. Each convent was, in this respect, a smaller St. Sophia; and every man who laid up gold and jewels in such a bank could sleep in peace.

"You must understand," said the Antiquary of

Novgorod, as we paddled in our boat down the Volkhoff, "that in ancient times, a convent was a home—a Family house. A man who made money by trade was minded in his old age to retire from the city and end his days in peace. In England such a man would buy him a country-house in the neighbourhood of his native town, in which he would live with his wife and children until he died. In a country like Old Russia, with brigands always at his gates, the man who saved money had to put his wealth under the protection of his church. Selecting a pleasant site, he would build his house in the name of his patron saint, adorn it with an altar, furnish it with a kitchen, dormitory, and cellar, and taking with him his wife, his children, and his pope, would set up his tent in that secure and comfortable place for the remainder of his days on earth."

"Could such a man have his wife and children near him?"

"Near him! With him; not only in his chapel but in his cell. The convent was his home—his country-house; and at his death descended to his son, who had probably become a monk. In some such fashion, many of the prettiest of these smaller convents on the Volkhoff came to be."

Half the convents in Great Russia were established as country-houses; the other half as Deserts—like Solovetsk; and many a poor fellow toiled like Zosima who has not been blessed with Zosima's fame.

But such a thing is possible, even now; for Russia has not yet passed beyond the legendary and heroic periods of her growth. The latest case is that of the new Desert founded at Gethsemane, on the plateau of the Troitsa, near Moscow; one of the most singular notes of the present time.

In the year 1803 was born in a log cabin, in a small village called Prechistoe (Very Clean), near the city of Vladimir, a male serf, so obscure that his family name has perished. For many years he lived on his lord's estate, like any other serf, marrying in his own class (twice), and rearing three strapping sons. At thirty-seven he was freed by his owner; when he moved from his village to Troitsa, took the name of Philip, put on cowl and gown, and dug for himself a vault in the earth. In this catacomb he spent five years of his life, until he found a more congenial home among the convent graves, where he lived for twenty years. Too fond of freedom to take monastic vows, he never placed himself under convent rule. Yet seeing, in spite of the proverb, that the hood makes the monk in Russia, if not elsewhere, he robed his limbs in coarse serge, girdled his waist with a heavy chain, and walked to the palace of Philaret, Metropolite of Moscow, begged that dignitary's blessing, and craved permission to adopt his name. Philaret took a fancy to the mendicant; and from that time forth the whilom serf from Very Clean was known in every street as Philaret-oushka —Philaret the Less.

Those graveyards of the Troitsa lay in a pretty and silent spot on the edge of a lake, enclosed in dark green woods. Among those mounds the mendicant made his Desert. Buying a few images and crosses in Troitsa and Gethsemane at two kopeks a-piece, he carried them into the streets and houses of Moscow; where he gave them to people, with his blessing; taking, in exchange, such gifts as his penitents pleased; a ruble, ten rubles, a hundred rubles each. He very soon had money in the bank. His images brought more rubles than his crosses; for his followers found that his images gave them luck, while his crosses sent them trouble. Hence a woman to whom he gave a cross went home with a heavy heart. Unlike the practice in Western countries, no peasant woman adorns herself with this memorial of her faith; nor is the cross a familiar ornament even in mansions of the rich. A priest wears a cross; a spire is crowned by a cross; but this symbol of our salvation is rarely seen among the painted and plated icons in a private house. To "bear the cross" is to suffer pain, and no one wishes to suffer pain. One cross a man is bound to bear—that hung about his neck at the baptismal font; but few men care to carry a second weight.

An oddity in dress and speech, Philaret-oushka wore no shoes and socks, and his greeting in the market was, "I wish you a merry Angel's day," instead of "I wish you well." In his Desert, and in his rambles, he was attended by as strange an oddity as himself; one Ivanoushka, John the Less. This man was never known to speak; he only sang. He sang in his cell; he sang on the road; he sang by the Holy Gate. The tone in which he sang reflected his master's mood; and the voice of John the Less told many a poor creature whether Philaret the Less would give her that day an image or a cross.

This mendicant had much success in merchants' shops. The more delicate ladies shrank from him with loathing, not because he begged their money, but because he defiled their rooms. Though born in Very Clean, this serf was dirtier than a monk; but his followers saw in his rusty chains, his grimy skin, his unkempt hair, so many signs of grace. The women of the trading classes courted him. A lady told me, that on calling to see a female friend, the wife of a merchant of the First Guild, she found her kneeling on the floor, and washing this beggar's feet. Her act was not a form; for the mendicant wore no shoes, and the streets of Moscow are foul with mire and hard with flints. One old maid, Miss Seribrikof, used to boast, as the glory of her life, that she had once been allowed to wash the good man's sores. Young brides would beg him to attend their nuptial feasts; at which he would "prophesy," as they call it; hinting darkly at their future of weal or woe. Sometimes he made a lucky hit. One day, at the wedding feast of Gospodin Sorokine, one of the richest men in Moscow, he turned to the bride and said, "When your feastings are over, you will have to smear your husband with honey." No one knew what he meant until three days later, when Sorokine died; on which event every one remembered that honey is tasted at all Russian funerals; and the words of Philaret the Less were likened to that Vision of Zosima which has since been painted on the pillar in Novgorod the Great.

Madame Loguinof, one of his rich disciples,

gave this mendicant money enough to build a church and convent, and when these edifices were raised in the graveyard of Troitsa, his "desert" was complete.

At the age of sixty-five this idol of the people passed away. When his high patron died, Philaret the Less was not so happy in his desert as of yore; for Innocent, the new Metropolite, was a real missionary of his faith, and not a man to look with favour on monks in masquerade. Deserting his desert, the holy man went his way from Troitsa into the province of Tula, where, in the village of Tcheglovo, he built a second convent, in which he died about a year ago. The two convents built by his rusty chains and dirty feet are now occupied by bodies of regular monks.

In these morbid growths of the religious sentiment, the Black Clergy seek support against the scorn and malice of a reforming world.

These monks have great advantages on their side. If liberal thought and science are against them, usage and repute are in their favour. All the high places are in their gift; all the chief forces are in their hands. The women are with them; and the ignorant rustics are mostly with them. Monks have always attracted the sex from which they fly; and every city in the empire has some story of a favourite Father followed, like Philaret the Less, by a female crowd. Vicar Nathaniel was not worshipped in the Nevski Prospect with a softer flattery than is Bishop Leonidas in the Kremlin gardens. Comedy but rarely touches these holy men; yet one may see in Moscow albums an amusing sketch of this gifted and fascinating man being lifted into higher place upon ladies' skirts.

The monks have not only got possession of the spiritual power; but they hold in their hands nearly all the sources of that spiritual power. They have the convents, catacombs, and shrines. They guard the bones of saints, and are themselves the stuff of which saints are made. In the golden book of the Russian Church there is not one instance of a canonized parish priest.

These celibate Fathers affect to keep the two great keys of influence in a land like Russia:—the Gift of Sacrifice, and the Gift of Miracles.

CHAPTER XVI.

Sacrifice.

SACRIFICE is a cardinal virtue of the Church. To the Russian mind it is the highest form of good; the surest sign of a perfect faith. Sacrifice is the evidence of a soul given up to God.

A child can only be received into the church through Sacrifice; and one of the forms in which a man gives himself up to Heaven is that of becoming insane "for the sake of Christ."

Last year (1868), a poor creature called Ivan Jacovlevitch died in the Lunatic Asylum in Moscow, after winning for himself a curious kind of fame. One half the world pronounced him mad; a second half respected him as a holy man. The first half, being the stronger, locked him up, and kept him under medical watch and ward until he died.

This Ivan, a burgher in the small town of Cherkesovo, made a "sacrifice" of his health and comfort to the Lord. By sacred vows, he bound himself never to wash his face and comb his hair, never to change his rags, never to sit on chair and stool, never to eat at table, never to handle knife and fork. In virtue of this Sacrifice, he lived like a dog; crouching on the floor, and licking up his food with lips and tongue. When brought into the madhouse, he was washed with soap and dressed in calico; but he began to mess himself on purpose; and his keepers soon gave up the task of trying to keep him clean.

No saint in the calendar draws such crowds to his shrine as Ivan Jacovlevitch drew to his chamber in this lunatic's house. Not only servant girls and farmers' wives, but women of the trading classes, came to him daily; bringing him dainties to eat, making him presents in money, and telling him all the secrets of their hearts. Sitting on the ground, and gobbling up his food, he stared at these visitors, mumbling some words between his teeth, which his listeners racked their brains to twist and frame into sense. He rolled the crumbs of his patties into pills, and when sick persons came to him to be cured, he put these dirty little balls into their mouths. This man was said to have become "insane for the Lord."

The authorities of the asylum lent him a spacious room, in which to receive his guests. They knew that he was mad; they knew that a crowded room was bad for him; but the public rush was so strong, that they could neither stand upon their science, nor enforce their rules. The lunatic died amidst the tears and groans of half the city. When the news of his death was noised abroad, a stranger would have thought the city was also mad. Men stopped in the street to kneel and pray; women threw themselves on the ground in grief; and a crowd of the lower classes ran about the bazaars and markets, crying, "Ivan is dead! Ivan is dead!

Ah! who will tell us what to do for ourselves now Ivan is 'dead?'"

On my table, as I write these words, lies a copy of the *Moscow Gazette*,—the journal which Katkoff edits, in which Samarin writes—containing a proposal, made by the clergy, for a public monument to Ivan Jacovlevitch, in the village where this poor lunatic was born!

All monks prefer to live a life of Sacrifice; the highest forms of Sacrifice being that of the Recluse and the Anchoret.

Every branch of the Oriental Church—Armenian, Coptic, Greek—encourages this form; but no Church on earth has given the world so many hermits as the Russ. Her calendar is full of anchorites, and the stories told of these self-denying men and women are often past belief. One Sister Maria was nailed up in a niche, at Hotkoff, fed through a hole in the rock, and lingered in her living tomb twelve years.

On the great plateau of the Troitsa, forty miles from Moscow, stands a monastic village, called Gethsemane. This monastic village is divided into two parts; the convent and the catacombs; separated by a black and silent lake.

A type of poverty and misery, the convent is built of rough logs, coloured with coarse paint. Not a trace of gold or silver is allowed, and the only ornaments are of cypress. Gowns of the poorest serge, and food of the simplest kind, are given to the monks. No female is allowed to enter this holy place, excepting once a-year, on the feast of the Virgin's ascent into heaven. Three women were standing humbly at the gate as we drove in; perhaps wondering why their sex should be shut out of Gethsemane, since their Lord was not betrayed in the garden by a female kiss!

Across the black lake lie the catacombs, cut off from the convent by a gate and fence; for into these living graves it is lawful for a female to descend. Deep down from the light of day, below the level of that sombre lake, these catacombs extend. We light each man his taper, as we stand above the narrow opening into the vaults. A monk, first crossing his breast and muttering his pass-words in an unknown tongue, goes down the winding stairs. We follow slowly, one by one, in silence; shading the light and holding to the wall. A faint smell fills our nostrils; a dull sound greets our ears; heavily comes our breath in the damp and fetid air. The tapers faint and flicker in the gloom. Gaining a passage, we observe some grated windows, narrow holes, and iron-bound doors. These openings lead into cells. The roof above is wet with slime, the floor is foul with crawling, nameless things.

"Hush!" drones the monk, as he creeps past some grated window and some ironclad door, as though he were afraid that we should wake the dead.

"What is this hole in the stone?" The monk stops short and waves his lurid light:—"A cell; a good man lies here; hush! his soul is now with God!"

"Dead?"

"Yea—dead to the world."

"How long has he been here?"

"How long?—Eleven years and more."

Passing this living tomb with a shiver, we catch the boom of a bell, and soon emerge from the narrow passage into a tiny church. A lamp is burning before the shrine; two monks are kneeling, with their temples on the floor; a priest is singing in a low, dull tone. The fittings of this church are all of brass; for pine and birch would rot into paste in a single year. Beyond the chapel we come to the holy well, the water of which is said to be good for body and soul. It is certainly earthy to the taste.

On coming into the light of day, we question the Fathers sharply as to that recluse who is said to have lived eleven years behind the ironclad door; and learn without surprise that he comes out from time to time, to ring the convent-bell, to fetch in wood, and hear the news! We learn that a man retired with his son into one of these catacombs; that he remained in his grave—so to speak—two years and a half, and then came out completely broken in his health. My eminent Russian friend, Professor Kapoustin, turns to me and says, "When our country was covered with forests, when our best road was a rut, and our villages were all shut in, a man who wished for peace of mind might wall himself up in a cell; but the country is now open, monks read newspapers, travellers come and go, and the Recluse likes to hear the news and see the light of day."

Instead of living in their catacombs, the monks now turn a penny by showing them to pilgrims, at the price of a taper, and by selling to visitors the portraits of monks and nuns who lived in the sturdier days of their church.

The spirit of Sacrifice takes other and milder forms. In the court-yards of Solovetsk one sees a strange creature, dressed in rags, fed on garbage, and lodged in gutters, who belongs to the monastic order, without being vowed as a regular monk. He lives by sufferance, not by right. He offers himself up as a daily sacrifice. He follows, so to speak, the calling of abjectness; and makes himself an example of the worthlessness of earthly things. This strange being is much run after by the poorer pilgrims, who regard him as a holy man; and he is noticeable as a type of what the Black clergy think meritorious in the Christian life.

Father Nikita, the name by which this man is known, is a dwarf, four feet ten inches high, with thin, grey beard, black face, and rat-like eyes. He never pollutes his skin with water and soap; for what is man that he should foster pride of the flesh? His garb is a string of rags and shreds; for he spurns the warmer and more decent habit of a monk. Instead of going to the store when he needs a frock, he crawls into the waste closet, where he begs as a favour that the Father having charge of the castaway clothes will give him the tatters which some poor brother has thrown aside. A room is left for his use in the cloister; but a bench of wood and a pillow of straw are things too good for dust and clay; and in token of his unworthiness, he lives on the open quay and sleeps in the convent yard.

Nobody can persuade him to sit down to the common meal; the sup of sour quass, the pound of black bread, the morsel of salt cod, being far too sumptuous food for him; but when the meal is over, and the crumbs are swept up, he will slink into the pantry, scrape into one dish the slops and bones, and make a repast of what peasants and beggars have thrown away.

He will not take his place in church; he will not pass through the Sacred Gates. When service is going on, he crouches in the darkest corner of the church, and listens to the prayers and chants with his head upon the ground. He likes to be spurned and buffeted by the crowd. A servant of every one, he is only too happy if folk will order him about; and when he can find a wretch so poor and dirty that every one else shuns him, he will take that dirty wretch to be his lord. In winter, when the snow lies deep on the ground, he will sleep in the open yard; in summer, when the heat is fierce, he will expose his shaven crown to the sun. He loves to be scorned, and spat upon, and robbed. Like all his class, he is fond of money; and this love of dross he turns into his sharpest discipline of soul. Twisting plaits of birch-bark into creels and crates, he vends these articles to boatmen and pilgrims at two kopeks a-piece; ties the copper coins in a filthy rag; and then creeps away to hide his money under a stone, in the hope that some one will watch him and steal it when he is gone.

The first monk who held the chair of Abjectness

in Solovetsk, before Nikita came in, was a miracle of self-denial, and his death was commemorated by an act of the rarest grace. Father Nahum is that elder and worthier Sacrifice to Heaven.

Nahum is said to have been more abject in manner, more self-denying in habit, than Nikita; being a person of higher order, and having more method in his scheme of Sacrifice. He abstained from the refuse of fish, as too great a delicacy for sinful men. He liked to sleep in the snow. He was only too happy to lie down at a beggar's door. Once, when he slept outside the Convent gates all night, some humorous brother suggested that perhaps he had been looking out for girls; and on hearing of this ribald jest he stripped himself nearly naked, poked a hole in the ice, and sat down in the frozen lake until his feet were chilled to the bone. A wing of the Convent once took fire, and the monks began to run about with pails; but Nahum rolled a ball of snow in his palms and threw it among the flames; and as the tongues lapped higher and higher, he ran to the church, threw himself on the floor, and begged the Lord to put them out. Instantly, say the monks, the fire died down. An Archimandrite saw him groping in a garden for potatoes, tearing up the roots with his fingers. "That is cold work, is it not, Nahum?" asked his kindly chief. "Humph!" said the monk; "try it." When the present Emperor came to Solovetsk, and every one was anxious to do him service, Nahum walked up to him with a wooden cup, half full of dirty water, saying, "Drink; it is good enough."

When this professor of Abjectness died, he was honoured by his brethren with a special funeral, inside the Convent gates. He was buried in the yard, beneath the Cathedral dome; where all day long, in the pilgrim season, a crowd of people may be seen about the block of granite which marks his grave; some praying beside the stone, as though he were already a "friend of God," while others are listening to the stories told of this uncanonized saint. Only one other monk of Solovetsk has ever been distinguished by such a mark of grace. Time—and time only—now seems wanting to Father Nahum's glory. In another generation—if the Black Clergy hold their own—Nahum of Solovetsk, canonized already by the popular voice of monks and pilgrims, will be taken up in St. Isaac's Square, and raised by imperial edict to his heavenly seat.

CHAPTER XVII.

Miracles.

YET the Gift of Miracles is greater than the Gift of Sacrifice. The Black Clergy stand out for miracles; not in a mystical sense, but in a natural sense; not only in times long past, but in the present hour; not only in the dark and in obscure hamlets, but in populous places and in the light of day.

At Kief a friend drives me out to the Caves of Anton and Feodosie; where we find some men and women standing by the gates, expecting the Father who keeps the keys to bring them and unlock the doors. As these living Pilgrims occupy us more than the dead anchorets, we join this party, pay our five kopeks, light our tapers, and descend with them the rocky stairs into the vault. Candle in hand, an aged monk goes forward, muttering in the gloom; stopping for an instant, here and there, to show us, lying on a ledge of rock, some coffin muffled in a pall. We thread a mile of lanes, saluting saint on saint, and twice or thrice we come into dwarf chapels, in each of which a lamp burns dimly before a shrine. The women kneel; the men cross themselves and pray. Moving forward in the dark, we come upon a niche in the wall, covered by a curtain and a glass door, on the ledge of which stands a silver dish, a little water, and a human skull. Our pilgrims cross themselves and mutter a voiceless prayer, while the aged monk lays down his taper and unlocks the door. A woman sinks on her knees before the niche, turns up her face, and shuts her eyes, while the Father, dipping a quill into the water, drops a little of the fluid on her eyelids. One by one, each pilgrim undergoes this rite; and then, on rising from his knees, lays down an offering of a few kopeks on the ledge of rock.

"What does this ceremony mean?" I ask the Father. "Mean?" says he: "a mystery—a miracle! This skull is the relic of a holy man whose eye had suffered from a blow. He called upon the Most Pure Mother of God; she heard his cry of pain; and in her pity she cured him of his wound."

"What is the name of that holy man?" "We do not know."

"When did he live and die?" "We do not know."

"Was he a monk of Kief?" "He was; and after he died his skull was kept, because his fame was great, and every one with pain in his eyes came hither to obtain relief."

Not one of our fellow-pilgrims has sore eyes; but who, as the Father urges, knows what the morrow may have in store? Bad eyes may come; and who would not like to ensure himself for ever against pain and blindness at the cost of five kopeks?

Such miracles are performed by the bones of saints in cities less holy and old than Kief.

Seraphim, a merchant of Kursk, abandoned his wife, his children, and his shop, to become a monk. Wandering to the cloister called the Desert of Sarof, in the province of Tambof, he dug for himself a hole in the ground, in which he lay down and slept. Some robbers came to his cave, where they beat and searched him; but, on finding his pockets empty, they knew that he must be a holy man. From that lucky day his fame spread rapidly abroad; and people came to see him from far and near; bringing presents of bread, of raiment, and of money; all of which he took into his cave, and doled out afterwards to the poor. A second window had to be cut into his cell; at one he received gifts, at the other he dispensed them. His Desert became a populous place, and the convent of Sarof grew into vast repute.

Seraphim founded a second Desert for women, ten miles distant from his own. A gentleman gave him a piece of ground; merchants sent him money; for his favour was by that time reckoned as of higher value than house and land. Lovely and wealthy women drove to see him, and to stay with him; entering into the Desert which he formed for them, and living apart from the world, without taking on their heads the burthen of conventual vows. At length a miracle was announced. A lamp which hung in front of a picture of the Virgin died out while Seraphim was kneeling on the ground; the chapel grew dark and the face of the Virgin faint; the pilgrims were much alarmed; when, to the surprise of every one who saw it, a light came out from the picture and re-lit the lamp! A second miracle soon followed. One day, a crowd of poor people came to the Desert for bread, when Seraphim had little in his cell to give. Counting his loaves, he saw that he had only two; and how was he to divide two loaves among all those hungry folk? He lifted up his voice—and lo! not two, but twenty loaves were standing on his board. From that time wonders were reported every year from Sarof; cures of all kinds; and the court in front of Seraphim's cell was thronged by the lame and blind, the deaf and dumb, by day and night.

Seraphim died in 1833; yet miracles are said to be effected at his tomb to this very hour. Already called a saint, the people ask his canonization from the Church. Every new Emperor makes a saint; as in Turkey every new Sultan builds a mosque; and Seraphim is fixed upon by the public voice as the man whom Alexander the Third will have to make a Saint.

One Motovilof, a landowner in the province of Penza, lame, unable to walk, applied for help to Seraphim, who promised the invalid, on conditions, a certain cure. Motovilof was to become a friend of Sarof; a supporter of the female Desert. Yielding to these terms, he was told to go down to Voronej, and to make his reverence at the shrine of Metrofanes, a local saint, on which he would find himself free from pain. Motovilof went to Voronej, and came back cured. With grateful heart he gave Seraphim a patch of land for his female Desert; and then, being busy with his affairs, he gradually forgot his pilgrimage and his miraculous cure. The pain came back into his leg; he could hardly walk; and not until he sent a supply of bread and clothes to Seraphim, was he restored in health. Not once, but many times, the worldly man was warned to keep his pledge; a journey to the Desert became a habit of his life; until he fell into love for one of Seraphim's fair penitents, and taking her home from her refuge, made that recluse his wife.

More noticeable still is the story of Tikhon, sometime Bishop of Voronej, now a recognised saint of the Orthodox Church. Tikhon is the official saint of the present reign; the living Emperor's contribution to the heavenly ranks.

Timothy Sokolof, son of a poor Reader in a village church, was born (in 1724) in that province of Novgorod which has given to Russia most of her popular saints. The Reader's family was large, his income small, and Timothy was sent to work on a neighbour's farm. Toiling in the fields by day, in the sheds by night; sleeping little, eating less; he yet contrived to learn how to read and write. Sent from this farm to a school, just opened in Novgorod, he toiled so patiently at his tasks, and made such progress in his studies, that on finishing his course he was appointed master of the school.

His heart was not in this work of teaching. From his cradle he had been fond of singing hymns and hearing mass, of being left alone with his books and thoughts, of flying from the face of man and the allurements of the world. A Vision shaped for him his future course. "When I was yet a teacher in the school," he said to a friend in after-life, "I sat up whole nights, reading and thinking. Once, when I was sitting up in May, the air being very soft, the sky very bright, I left my cell, and stood under the starry dome, admiring the lights, and thinking of our eternal life. Heaven opened to my sight—a Vision such as human words can never paint! My heart was filled with joy, and from that hour I felt a passionate longing to quit the world."

A few years after he took the cowl and changed the name of Timothy for Tikhon, he was raised from his humble cell to the Episcopal bench; first in Novgorod, afterwards at Voronej; the second a missionary see; the province of Voronej lying close to the Don Kozak country and the Tartar steppe.

The people of this district were lawless tribes; Kozaks, Kalmuks, Malo-Russ; a tipsy, idle, vagabond crew; the clergy worse, it may be, than their flocks. Voronej had no schools; the popes could hardly read; the services were badly sung and said. All classes of the people lived in sin. Tikhon began a patient wrestle with these disorders. Opening with the priests, and with the schools, he put an end to flogging in the seminaries; in order, as he said, to raise the standing of a priest, and cause the student to respect himself. This change was but a sign of things to come. By easy steps he won his clergy to live like priests; to drink less, to pray more; and generally to act as ministers of God. In two years he purged the schools and purified the Church.

No less care was given to lay disorders. Often he had to be plain in speech; but such was the reverence felt for him by burgher and peasant that no one dared to disregard his voice. "You must do so if Tikhon tells you," they would say to each other; "if not, he will complain of you to God." He dressed in a coarse robe; he ate plain food; he sent the wine untouched from his table to the sick. He was the poor man's friend; and only waited on the rich when he found no wretched ones at his gates. The power of Tikhon lay in his faultless life, in his tender tones, and in his loving heart. "Want of love," he used to urge, "is the cause of all our misery; had we more love for our brothers, pain and grief would be more easy to bear; love soothes away all grief and pain."

Two years in Novgorod, five years in Voronej, he spent in these gracious labours, till the longing of his heart for solitude grew too strong. Laying down his mitre, he retired from his palace in Voronej to the convent of Zadonsk, a little town on the river Don, where he gave up his time to writing tracts and visiting the poor. These labours were of highest use; for Tikhon was among the first (if not the first of all) to write in favour of the Serf. Fifteen volumes of his works are printed; fifteen more are said to lie in manuscript; and some of these works have gone through fifty editions from the Russian press.

Tikhon's great merit as a writer lies in the fact that he foresaw, prepared, and urged, Emancipation of the Serfs.

For fifteen years he lived the life of a holy man. As a friend of serfs, he one day went to the house of a prince, in the district of Voronej, to point out some wrong which they were suffering on his estate, and to beg him, for the sake of Jesus and Mary, to be tender with the poor. The prince got angry with his guest for putting the thing so plainly into words; and in the midst of some sharp speech between them, struck him in the face. Tikhon rose up and left the house; but when he had walked some time, he began to see that he—no less than his host—was in the wrong. This man, he said to himself, has done a deed, of which, on cooling down, he will feel ashamed. Who has caused him to do that wrong? "It was my doing," sighed the reprover, turning on his heel, and going straight back into the house. Falling at the prince's feet, Tikhon craved his pardon for having stirred him into wrath and caused him to commit a sin. The man was so astonished, that he knelt down by the monk, and kissing his hands, implored his forgiveness and 'his benediction. From that hour, it is said, the prince was another man; noticeable through all the province of Voronej for his kindness to the serfs.

Tikhon lived into his eightieth year. Before he passed away, he told the brethren of his convent he would live until such a day and then depart. He died, as he had told them he should die; on the day foreseen, and in the midst of his weeping friends. From the day of his funeral, his shrine in Zadonsk was visited by an ever-increasing crush; for cures of many kinds were wrought; the sick recovered, the lame walked home, the blind saw, the crooked became straight. A thousand voices claimed the canonization of this Friend of Serfs; until the reigning Emperor, struck by this appeal, invited the Holy Governing Synod to conduct the inquiries which precede the canonization of a Russian Saint.

The commission sat; the miracles were proved; and then the tomb was opened. Out from the coffin came a scent of flowers; the flesh was pure and sweet; and the act of canonization was decreed and signed in 1861, the Emancipation year. Tikhon of Zadonsk is the Emancipation Saint.

Yet, according to the Black Clergy, the newest and the greatest miracle of modern times is the Virgin's defence of Solovetsk against the Anglo-French squadron in 1854.

The wardrobe of Solovetsk contains the chief treasures of the cloister; old charters and letters; original grants of lands; the rescript of Peter; manuscript lives of Savatie and Zosima; service-books, richly bound in golden plates; Pojarski's sword; cups, lamps, crosses, candlesticks in gold and silver; but the treasure of treasures is the evidence of that stupendous miracle, wrought by the Most Pure Mother of God.

On the centre stand, under a glass case, strongly locked, lie an English shell and two round shot.

They are carefully inscribed. A reliquary in a closet holds a dozen bits of brass, the rent fusees of exploded shells. A number of prints are sold to the devout, in which the English gun-boats are moored under the Convent wall, so near that men might easily have leaped on shore. Among this mass of evidence is a new and splendid Sacramental cup; the gift of Russia to Solovetsk—in memory of the day when human help had failed, and "the Convent that endureth for ever" was saved by the Virgin Mother of God.

A scoffer here and there may smile. "Savatie! Zosima!" laughed a Russian cynic in my face; "you English made the fortune of these saints. How so? You see a peasant has but two notions in his pate; the Empire and the Church; a power of the flesh and a power of the spirit. Now, see what you have done. You wage war upon us; you send your fleets into the Black Sea and into the White Sea; in the first to fight against the Empire, in the second to fight against the Church. In one sea, you win; in the other sea, you lose. Sevastopol falls to your arms; while Solovetsk drives away your ships. The arm of the spirit is seen to be stronger than the arm of flesh. What then? 'Heaven,' says the rustic to his neighbour as they dawdle home from church, 'is mightier than the Tsar.' For fifty years to come our superstitions will lie on English heads!"

The tale of that miracle, told me on the spot, will sound in some ears like a piece of high comedy, in others like a chapter from some ancient and forgotten book. A dry despatch from Admiral Ommanney contains the little that we know of our "Operations in the White Sea;" the next chapter gives the story, as they tell it on the other side.

CHAPTER XVIII.

The Great Miracle.

So soon as news arrived in the Winter Palace that an English fleet was under steam for the Polar seas, the War Office set to work in the usual way; sending out arms and men; such arms and men as could be found and spared in these Northern towns. Six old siege guns, fit for a museum, were shipped from Archangel to the Convent, with five artillerymen, and fifty troopers of the line, selected from the Invalid Corps. An officer came with these forces to conduct the defence.

Just as the English ships were entering on their task this officer died (June, 1854); no doubt by the hand of God, in order to rebuke the pride of man, while adding fresh lustre to the auriol of His saints. The arm of flesh having failed, the Fathers threw themselves on the only Power that can never fail.

Father Alexander, then the Archimandrite, ordered a series of services to be held in the several chapels within the walls. A special office was appointed for Sunday; with a separate appeal to Heaven for guidance; first in the name of the Most Sweet Infant Jesus; afterwards in that of the Most Pure Mother of God. Midnight services were also given; the effect of which is said to have been great and strange; firing the monks with a new and wonderful spirit of confidence in their cause. The Archimandrite sang mass in person before the tombs of Savatie and Zosima, in the crypt of the cathedral church, and also before the miracle-working picture of the Virgin brought by Savatie to his desert. This picture—so important in the story—came from Greece. The service sung before it filled the monks with gladness; warmth and comfort flowed from the Madonna's face; and her adorers felt themselves conquerors, in her name, before the English warships hove in sight.

In their first trouble, the copes and missals, charters and jewels, had been sent away into the inland towns. This act of doubt occurred before the officer died, and the monks had taken upon themselves the burthen of defence. To those who carried away the cups and crosses, robes and books, the Archimandrite gave his blessing and his counsel. "Know," he said to them at parting, "that, whether you be on sea or land, that every Friday we shall be fasting and praying for you; do you the same; and God will preserve the things which belong to His service, and which you are carrying away; follow my commands, and come back to me in a better time, sound in health, with the things of which you go in charge." When news came in that English ships were cruising off the bar of Archangel, some of the brethren fainted; "left by the Emperor," they sighed, "to be made a sacrifice for his sins." Ten days before the squadron came in sight, the Archimandrite held a service in his church to encourage these feeble souls; and when his prayers were ended, he addressed them thus: "Grieve not that the defence seems weak while the foe is strong. Rely upon our Lord, upon His Most Pure Mother, upon the two excellent Saints who have promised that this Convent shall endure for ever. Jesus will perform a miracle, for their sake, such as the world has never seen." A ray of comfort stole into their hearts; and rolling out barrels of pitch and tar, they smeared the wooden shingles of wall and tower, filled pails of water in readiness to drench out fires, and took down from the Convent armoury the rusty pikes and bills which had been lying up since the attack of Swedish ships in the days of Peter the Great.

A hundred texts were found to show that these old weapons could be used again, even as the arms of David were used once more by the Lion of Judah in defence of Solomon's shrine. Young children came into the monastery from Kem and Suma; vowed by their fathers to the cause of God; and many old pikes and bills were put into these infant hands. "The fire of your ships," said one of the monks, "did not frighten these innocents, who played with the shells as though they had been harmless toys." Not a child was hurt.

When the fleet was signalled from the outlooks, Alexander spoke to his brethren after meat: "Have a good heart," he cried; "we are not weak, as we appear; for God is on our side. If we were saved by an army, where would be our credit? With the soldiery, with the world! What would be our gain? But if, by prayer alone, we drive the squadron from our shores, the glory will belong to our Convent and our faith. Have a good heart! Slava Bogu—Glory to God!"

On Tuesday morning (July 18th, 1854) the watchers signalled two frigates, which were rounding Beluga Point:—the Archimandrite proclaimed a three days' fast. The two frigates anchored seven miles from the shore:—the Archimandrite ordered the Convent-bell to toll for a special service to the Most Pure Mother of God. Like a Hebrew king, he took off his gorgeous robes, and humbling himself before the Fathers, read a prayer in front of the tombs of Savatie and Zosima, and, taking down the miraculous picture of the Virgin, marched with it in procession round the walls. Then—but not till then—the frigates sailed away.

As the ships steamed off towards Kem, it was feared they might still come back; and Ensign Niconovitch, commanding the Company of Invalids, went out to survey the shores, dragging two three-pounder guns through the sand; while many of the Pilgrims and workmen offered their services as scouts. Niconovitch built a battery of sods and sand, behind which he trained his guns; and eight small pieces were laid upon the towers and walls, after which the Fathers fell once more to prayer.

Next day a trail of smoke was seen in the summer sky. The two ships, soon known to them as the "Brisk" and the "Miranda," steamed into the bay. The "Brisk," say the monks, was the first to speak, and she opened her parley with a rattling shot. Standing on the quay, the Archimandrite was nearly struck by a ball, and his people, frightened at the crashing roar, ran up into the Convent-yard, and tried to close behind them the Sacred Gates.

A petty officer, one Drushlevski, having charge of ten men and a gun in the Weaver's tower, returned the fire; on which the English frigate is said to have opened her broadside on the tower and wall. Drushlevski took up her challenge; but with aim and prudence, having very little powder in his casks. The "Brisk," they say, fired thirty rounds, while the officer in the Weaver's tower discharged his gun three times. The English frigate then sheered off; a shot from the Convent gun having struck her side, and killed a man.

That night was spent in joy and prayer. The Archimandrite kissed Drushlevski, and gave his blessing to every gunner in the Weaver's tower. When night came on—the summer night of the Frozen Sea—the frigates were out of sight; but no one felt secure, and least of all Drushlevski, that this triumph of the cross was yet complete. Not a soul in the Convent slept.

Dawn brought them one of the holiest festivals of the Russian year; Thursday, July 20th, the feast of Our Lady of Kazan; a day on which no plough is driven, no mill is opened, no school is kept, in any part of Russia, from the White Sea to the Black. Matins were sung, as usual, in the Cathedral Church at half-past two; the Archimandrite steadily going through his chant, as though the peril were not nigh. Te Deum was just being finished, when a boat came ashore from the "Brisk," carrying a white flag, and bringing a summons for the Convent to yield her keys. The letter was in English, accompanied by a bad translation, in which the word for "squadron of ships" was rendered by the Russian term for squadron of horse. Consulting with his monks—who laughed in good hearty mood at the idea of being set upon by cavalry from the sea—the Archimandrite told the messenger to say his answer should be sent to the "Brisk" by an officer of his own.

Two "insolent conditions" were imposed by the Admiral: (1.) The commander was to yield his sword in person; (2.) The garrison were to become prisoners of war. Ommanney's letter informed the Fathers that if a gun were fired from the wall, his bombardment would begin at once; alleging in explanation that on the previous day, a gun in the Convent had opened on his ship.

One Soltikoff, a Pilgrim, carried the Archimandrite's answer to the "Brisk:"—a proud refusal to give up his keys. Denying that the Convent had opened fire on the English boat, he said the first shot came from the frigate, and the Convent simply replied to it in self-defence. The paper was unsigned; the monk declaring that as a man of peace he could not write his name on a document treating of blood and death.

Admiral Ommanney told the Pilgrim there was nothing more to say; the bombardment would begin at once; and the Convent would be swept from the earth. Soltikoff asked for time, and Ommanney offered him three hours' grace. It was now five in the morning, and the Admiral gave the Fathers until eight o'clock; but on the Pilgrim saying the time was short, Ommanney is said to have sworn a great oath, and lessened his term of grace three-quarters of an hour. He kept his oath; the bombardment opened at a quarter to eight o'clock, of that holy day—inscribed to Our Lady of Kazan—our Lady of Victory; the first shell flying over the Convent shingles, almost as soon as Soltikoff reached the Sacred Gates.

On the English frigates opening fire, the bell in the court-yard tolled the monks to prayer. Shot, shell, grenade and cartridge rained on the walls and domes; yet the services went on all day; a hurricane of fire without; an agony of prayer within! While the people were on their knees, a shell struck the Cathedral dome—the rent of which is piously preserved—and tearing through the wooden frame-work, dashed down the ceiling on the supplicants' heads. The rafters were on fire; the church was suddenly filled with smoke. A sacred image was grazed and singed. The windows cracked; the doors flew open; the buildings reeled and shivered; and the terrified people fell with their faces on the stones. One man only kept his feet. Standing before the royal gates, the Archimandrite cried: "Stay! stay! Be not afraid, the Lord will guard His own!" The monks and pilgrims, lifting up their eyes, beheld the old man standing before his altar, quiet and erect, with big tears rolling down his cheeks. They sprang to their feet; they ran to fetch water; they put out the flames;

they swept off the wreck of dust and rafters; and when the floor was cleansed, they sank on their knees and bowed their heads once more in prayer.

When mass was over, three poor women remained in the Cathedral on their knees; a shell came through the roof, and burst; on which the poor things crawled toward the shrines where men were praying, and women are not allowed to come. A good pope let them in, and suffered them to pray with the men; an act which the monks regard as one of the highest wonders of that miraculous day.

A petty officer named Ponomareff occupied with his gun a spit of rock, from which he could tease the frigates, and draw upon himself no little of their wrath. Every shot from the "Miranda" splashed the mire about his men, who were often buried, though they were not killed that day. Leaping to his feet, and shaking the dirt from his clothes, Ponomareff stood to his gun, until he was called away. He and three other men crept through the stones and trees, to places far apart; whence they discharged their carbines, and ran away into the scrub, after drawing upon these points a rattle of shot and shell. At length, he was recalled. "It is a sad day for the monastery," sighed the gunner, "but we are willing to die with the saints."

Services were sung all day in front of the shrines of Savatie and Zosima. Once a shot struck the altar; the pope shrank back from his desk; and the people fell on their faces. Every one supposed that his hour was come, and many cried out in their fear for the bread and wine. Father Varnau, the confessor, took his seat, confessed the people, and gave them the sacrament. Alexander was the first to confess his sins, and make up his account with God. The elders followed; then the lay-monks, pilgrims, soldiers, women; and when all were shriven, the body of penitents pressed around the shrines of Philip, Savatie, Zosima, and the Mother of God.

A little after noon, the Convent-bells in the yard were tolled, the monks and pilgrims gathered on the wall, and lines of procession were ordered to be formed. The monks stood first, the pilgrims next, the women and children last; and when they were all got ready to march, the Archimandrite took down from the screen beside his altar the Miraculous Virgin and the principal cross; and placing himself in front of his people, with the cross in his right hand, the Virgin in his left, conducted them round the ramparts under fire. He waved his cross, and blessed the Pilgrims with the Miraculous Virgin as he strode along. The great bell tolled, the monks and pilgrims sang a psalm. Shot and shell rained overhead; the boulders trembled in the wall; the shingles cracked and split on the roof. Near the corner tower by the Holy Lake, the procession came to a halt. A shell had struck the windmill, setting the fans on fire. Pealing their psalm, and calling on their saints, they waited till the flames died down, and then resumed their march. A shot came dashing through the rampart; splintering the logs and planks in their very midst; and cutting the line of procession into head and heel. "Advance!"

cried the Archimandrite, waving his cross and picture, and the people instantly advanced. On reaching the Weaver's tower, from which the shot of destiny had been fired the previous day, the Archimandrite, calling the monk Gennadie to his side, gave him the cross, with orders to carry it up into the tower, and let the gunners kiss the image of our Lord. While Gennadie was absent on this errand, the Archimandrite showed the monks and pilgrims that the Convent doves were not fluttered in their nests by the English guns.

A miracle! When the procession moved from the Weaver's tower, they came near some open ground, which they were obliged to cross, under showers of shot. No man of flesh and blood—unless protected from on high—could pass through that fire unscathed. But now was the time to try men's faith. A moment only the procession paused; the Archimandrite, holding up his miraculous picture of the Mother of God, advanced into the cloud of dust and smoke; the people pealed their psalm; and the shells and balls from the English ships were seen to curve in their flight, to whirl over dome and tower, and come down splashing into the Holy Lake! Every eye saw that miracle; and every heart confessed the Most Pure Mother of God.

The frigates then drew off, and went their way; to be seen from the watch-towers of the sacred isles no more; vanquished and put to shame; though visibly not by the hand of man. Not a soul in the Convent had been hurt; though hurricanes of brass and iron had been fired from the English decks.

A Norwegian named Harder, a visitor by chance at Solovetsk, was so much struck by this miraculous defence, that he cried in the Convent-yard, "How great is the Russian God!" and begged to be admitted a member of their Church.

The news of this attack by an English Admiral on Solovetsk was carried into every part of Russia, and the effect which it produced on the Russian mind may be conceived by any one who will take the pains to imagine how he would feel on hearing reports from Palestine that a Turkish Pasha had opened fire on the dome and cross of the Holy Sepulchre. Shame, astonishment, and fury filled the land, until the further news arrived that this abominable raid among the holy graves and shrines had come to nought. Since that year of miracles, young and old, rich and poor, have come to regard a journey to Solovetsk as only second in merit to a voyage to Bethlehem and the Tomb of Christ. Peasants set the fashion, which Emperors and Grand Dukes are taking up. Alexander the Second has made a pilgrimage to these holy isles; his brother Constantine has done the same; and two of his sons will make the trip next year. The Empress, too, is said to have made a vow, that if Heaven restores her strength she will pay a visit to Savatie's shrine.

Some people think these visits of the imperial race are due, not only to the wish to lead where they might otherwise have to follow, but to matters connected with that mystery of a buried Grand Duke which lends so dark a fame to the Convent in the Frozen Sea.

CHAPTER XIX.

A Convent Spectre.

A LAND alive with goblins and sorceries, in which every monk sees visions, in which every woman is thought to be a witch, presents the proper scenery for such a legend as that of the Convent Spectre, called the Spirit of the Frozen Sea.

Faith in the existence of this phantom is widely spread. I have met with evidences of this faith not only in the Northern seas, but on the Volga, in hamlets of the Ukraine, and among Old Believers in Moscow, Novgorod, and Kief. All the Ruthenians, most of the Don Kozaks, and many of the Poles, give credit to this tale, in either a spiritualised or physical form.

Rufin Pietrowski, the Pole who escaped from his Siberian mine, and crossing the Ural Mountains, dropped down the river Dvina on a raft, and got as near to Solovetsk as Onega Point, reports the spectre as a fact, and offers the explanation which was given of it by his fellow-pilgrims. He says it is not a ghost, but a living man. Other and later writers than Pietrowski hint at such a mystery; but the tale is one of which men would rather whisper in corners than prate in books.

"You have been to Solovetsk?" exclaimed to me a native of Kalatch, on the Don, a man of wit and spirit. "May I ask whether you saw anything there that struck you much?".

"Yes, many things; the Convent itself, the farms and gardens, the dry dock, the fishing-boats, the salt-pits, the tombs of saints."

"Ah! yes, they would let you see all those things; but they would not let you go into their secret prison."

"Why not?" I said, to lead him on.

"They have a prisoner in that building whom they dare not show."

The same thing happened to me several times, with variations of time and place.

Some boatman from the Lapland ports, while striving, in the first hard days of winter, with the floes of ice, is driven beneath the fortress curtain, where he sees on looking up, in the faint light of dusk, a venerable figure passing behind a loop-hole in the wall; his white hair cut, which proves that he is not a monk; his eyes upraised to heaven; his hands clasped fervently, as though he were in prayer; his whole appearance that of a man appealing to the justice of God against the tyranny of man. A sentry passes the loop-hole, and the boatman sees no more.

This figure is not seen at other times and by other folk. Three months in the year these islands swarm with pilgrims, many of whom come and go in their craft from Onega and Kem. These visitors paddle below the ramparts day and night; yet nothing is seen by them of the aged prisoner and his sentry on the Convent wall. Clearly, then, if the figure is that of a living man, there must be reasons for concealing him from notice during the Pilgrim months.

"Hush!" said a boatman once to a friend of mine, as he lay in a tiny cove under the Convent wall; "you must not speak so loud; these rocks can hear. One dares not whisper in one's sleep, much less on the open sea, that the phantom walks yon wall. The pope tells you it is an imp; the elder laughs in your face and calls you a fool. If you believe your eyes they say you are crazed, not fit to pull a boat."

"You have not seen the figure?"

"Seen him—no; he is a wretched one, and brings a man bad luck. God help him . . . if he is yet alive!"

"You think he is a man of flesh and blood?"

"Holy Virgin keep us! who can tell?"

"When was he last seen?"

"Who knows? A boatman seldom pulls this way at dusk; and when he finds himself here by chance, he turns his eyes from the castle wall. Last year, a man got into trouble by his chatter. He came to sell his fish, and fetching a course to the south, brought up his yawl under the castle guns. A voice called out to him, and when he looked up suddenly, he saw behind the loop-hole a bare and venerable head. While he stood staring in his yawl, a crack ran through the air, and looking along the line of roof, he saw, behind a puff of smoke, a sentinel with his gun. A moment more and he was off. When the drink was in his head, he prated about the ghost, until the elder took away his boat and told him he was mad."

"What is the figure like?"

"A tall old man, white locks, bare head, and eyes upraised, as if he were trying to cool his brain."

"Does he walk the same place always?"

"Yes, they say so; always. Yonder—between the turrets, is the phantom's walk. Let us go back. Hist! That is the Convent-bell."

The explanation hinted by Pietrowski, and widely taken for the truth, is that the figure which walks these ramparts is the winter months, is not only that of a living man, but of a popular and noble prince; no less a personage than the Grand Duke Constantine, elder brother of the late Emperor Nicolas, and natural heir to the imperial crown!

This prince, in whose cause so many patriots lost their lives, is commonly supposed to have given up the world for love; to have willingly renounced his rights of succession to the throne; to have acquiesced in his younger brother's reign; to have died of cholera in Minsk; to have been buried in the fortress of St. Peter and St. Paul. But many persons look on this story as a mere official tale. Their version is, that the prince was a liberal prince; that he married for love; that he never consented to waive his rights of birth; that the documents published by the Senate were forged; that the Polish rising of 1831 was not directed against him; that the attack on his summer palace was a feint; that his retirement to Minsk was involuntary; that he did not die of cholera, as announced; that he was seized in the night, and whisked away in a tarantass, while Russia was deceived by funeral rites; that he was driven in the tarantass to Archangel, whence he was borne to Solovetsk; that he escaped from the Convent; that in the year of Emancipation he suddenly appeared in Penza; that he announced a reign of liberty and peace; that he was followed by thousands of peasants; that on being defeated by General Dreniakine, he was suffered to escape; that he was afterwards seized in secret, and sent back to Solovetsk; where he is still occasionally seen by fishermen walking on the Convent wall.

The facts which underlie these versions of the same historical events, are wrapped in not a little doubt; and what is actually known is of the kind that may be read in a different sense by different eyes.

CHAPTER XX.

Story of a Grand Duke.

WHEN Alexander the First — elder brother of Constantine and Nicolas — died, unexpectedly, at Taganrog, on the distant Sea of Azof, leaving no son to reign in his stead, the crown descended, by law and usage, to the brother next in birth. Constantine was then at Warsaw, with his Polish wife; Nicolas was at St. Petersburg, with his guards. Constantine was called the Heir; and up to that hour no one seems to have doubted that he would wear the crown, in case the Emperor's life should fail. There was, however, a party in the Senate and the barrack against him; the old Russian party, who could not pardon him his Polish wife.

When couriers brought the news from Taganrog to St. Petersburg, Nicolas, having formed no plans as yet, called up the guards, announced his brother's advent to the throne, and set them an example of loyalty by taking the oath of allegiance to his Imperial Majesty Constantine the First. The guards being sworn, the generals and staff-officers signed the act of accession and took the oaths. Cantering off to their several barracks, these officers put the various regiments of St. Petersburg under fealty to Constantine the First; and Nicolas sent news that night to Warsaw that the new Emperor had begun to reign.

But while the messengers were tearing through the winter snows, some members of the Senate came to Nicolas with yet more startling news. Alexander, they said, had left with them a sealed paper, contents unknown, which they were not to open until they heard that he was dead. On opening this packet, they found in it two papers; one a letter from the Grand Duke Constantine, written in 1822, renouncing his rights in the crown; the second, a manifesto by the dead Emperor, written in 1823, accepting that renunciation and adopting his brother Nicolas as his lawful heir. A similar packet, they alleged, had been secretly left with Philaret of Moscow, and would be found in the sacristy of his cathedral church. Nicolas scanned these documents closely; saw good reason to put them by; and urged the whole body of the Senate to swear fidelity to Constantine the First. In every office of the State the imperial functionaries took this oath. All Russia, in fact all Europe, saw that Constantine had opened his reign in peace.

Then followed a surprise. Some letters passed between the two Grand Dukes, in which (it was said) the brothers were each endeavouring to force the other to ascend the throne; Nicolas urging that Constantine was the elder born and rightful heir; Constantine urging that Nicolas had better health and a more active spirit. Ten days rolled by. The empire was without a chief. A plot, of which Pestel, Rostovtsef, and Mouravief, were leading spirits, was on the point of explosion. But on Christmas Eve, the Grand Duke Nicolas made up his mind to take the crown. He spent the night in drawing up a manifesto, setting forth the facts which led him to occupy his brother's seat; and on Christmas Day he read this paper in the Senate, by which body he was at once proclaimed Autocrat and Tsar. A hundred generals rode to the various barracks, to read the new proclamation, and to get those troops who had sworn but a week ago to uphold his Majesty Constantine the First, to cast that oath to the winds, and swear a second time to uphold his Majesty Nicolas the First. But, if most of the regiments were quick to unswear themselves by word of command, a part of the guards, and chiefly the marines and grenadiers, refused; and, marching from their quarters into St. Isaac's Square, took up a menacing position towards the new Emperor, while a cry rose wildly from the crowd, of "Long live Constantine the First!"

A shot was heard.

Count Miloradovitch, governor-general of St. Petersburg, fell dead; a brave general who had passed through fifty battles, killed as he was trying to harangue his troops. A line of fire now opened on the square. Colonel Stürler fell, at the head of his regiment of guards. When night came down, the ground was covered with dead and dying men; but Nicolas was master of the square. A charge of grape-shot swept the streets clear of rioters, just as night was coming down.

When the trials to which the events of that day gave rise came on, it suited both the government and the conspirators to keep the Grand Duke out of sight. Count Nesselrode told the courts that this revolt was revolutionary, not dynastic; and Nicolas denounced the leaders to his people as men who wished to bring "a foreign contagion upon their sacred soil."

The Grand Duke and his Polish wife remained in Warsaw, living at the summer garden of Belvedere, in the midst of woods and lakes, of pictures, and works of art. Once, indeed, he left his charming villa for a season; to appear, quite unexpectedly (the court declared) in the Kremlin, and assist in placing the Imperial crown on his brother's head. That act of grace accomplished, he returned to Warsaw; where he reigned as viceroy; keeping a modest court, and leading an almost private life. But the country was excited, the army was not content. One war was forced by Nicolas on Persia, a second on Turkey; both of them glorious for the Russian arms; yet men were said to be troubled at the sight of a younger brother on the throne; a sentiment of reverence for the elder son being one of the strongest feelings in a Slavonic breast; and all these troubles were kept alive by the social and political writhings of the Poles.

Two prosperous wars had made the Emperor so proud and haughty that when news came in from Paris, telling him of the fall of Charles the Tenth, he summoned his minister of war, and ordered his troops to march. He said he would move on Paris, and his Kozaks began to talk of picqueting their horses on the Seine. But the French have agencies of mischief in every town of Poland; and in less than five months after Charles the Tenth left Paris, Warsaw was in arms.

Every act of this Polish rising seems, so far as concerns the Grand Duke Constantine, to admit of being told in different ways.

A band of young men stole into the Belvedere in the gloom of a November night, and ravaged through the rooms. They killed General Gendre; they killed the Vice-President of Police, Lubowicki; and they suffered the Grand Duke to escape by the garden gate. These are the facts; but whether he escaped by chance is what remains in doubt. The Russian version was that these young fellows came to kill the prince, as well as Gendre and Lubowicki; that a servant, hearing the tumult near the palace, ran to his master's room, and led him through the domestic passages into the open air. The Polish version was, that these young men desired to find the prince; not to murder him, but to use him as either hostage or emperor in their revolt against his brother's rule.

Arriving in Warsaw from his country-house, the Grand Duke, finding that city in the power of a revolted soldiery, moved some posts on the road towards the Russian frontier. Agents came to assure him that no harm was meant to him; that he was free to march with his guards and stores; that no one would follow him or molest him on the road. Some Polish companies were with him; and four days after his departure from Belvedere, he received in his camp near Warsaw a deputation, sent to him by his own request, from the insurgent chiefs. Then came the act which roused the anger of his brother's court; and led, as some folk think, to the mystery and sympathy which cling around his name.

He asked the deputation to state their terms. "A living Poland!" they replied; "the charter of Alexander the First; a Polish army and police; the restoration of our ancient frontier." In return, he told these deputies that he had not sent to Lithuania for troops; and he consented that the Polish companies in his camp should return to Warsaw and join the insurgent bands! For such a surrender to the rebels any other general in the service would certainly have been tried and shot. The Emperor, when he heard the news, went almost mad with rage; and every one wishing to stand well at court began to whisper that the Grand Duke Constantine had forfeited his honour and his life.

Constantine died suddenly at Minsk. The disease was cholera; the corpse was carried to St. Petersburg; and the prince, who had lost a crown for love, was laid with honour among the ashes of his race, in the gloomy fortress of St. Peter and St. Paul.

But no gazetteer could make the common people believe that their prince was gone from them for ever. Like his father Paul, and like his grandfather Peter, he was only hiding in some secret place; and putting their heads together by the winter fires, they told each other he would come again.

In the Year of Emancipation (1861) a man appeared in the province of Penza, who announced himself not only as the Grand Duke, but as a prophet, a leader, and a messenger from the Tsar. He told the people they were being deceived by their priests and lords, that the Emperor was on their side, that the Emancipation Act gave them the land without purchase and rent-charge, and that they must support the Emperor in his design to do them good. A crowd of peasants, gathering to his voice, and carrying a red banner, marched through the villages, crying death tö the priests and nobles. General Dreniakine, an aide-de-camp of the Emperor, a prompt and confidential officer, was sent from St. Petersburg against the "Grand Duke," whom in his proclamation he called Egortsof; and after a smart affair, in which eight men were killed, and twenty-six badly hurt, the peasants fled before the troops. The "Grand Duke" was suffered to escape; and nothing more has been heard of him, except an official hint that he is dead.

What wonder that a credulous people fancies the hero of such adventures may be still alive!

In every country which has virtue enough to keep the memory of a better day, the popular mind is apt to clothe its hopes in this legendary form. In England, the commons expected Arthur to awake; in Portugal, they expected Sebastian to return; in Germany, they believed that Barbarossa sat on his lonely peak. Masses of men believe that Peter the Third is living, and will yet resume his throne.

Before landing in the Holy Isles, I gave much thought to this mystery of the Grand Duke, and nursed a very faint hope of being able to resolve the spectre into some mortal shape.

CHAPTER XXI.

Dungeons.

My mind being full of this story, I keep an eye on every gate and trap that might lead me either up or down into a prisoner's cell. My leave to roam about the convent-yards is free; and though I am seldom left alone, except when lodged in my private room, some chance of loitering round the ramparts falls in my way from time to time. The monks retire about seven o'clock, and as the sun sets late in the summer months, I stroll through the woods and round by the Holy Lake, while Father John is laying our supper of cucumbers and sprats. Sometimes I get a peep at strange places while the Fathers are at mass.

One day, when strolling at my ease, I come into a small court-yard, which my clerical guides have often passed by. A flutter of wings attracts me to the spot, and, throwing a few crumbs of biscuit on the ground, I am instantly surrounded by a thousand beautiful doves. They are perfectly tame. Here, then, is that colony of doves which the Archimandrite told his people were not disturbed by the English guns; and looking at the tall buildings and the narrow yard, I am less surprised by the miracle than when the story was told me by the monks. Lifting my eyes to the sills from which these birds come fluttering down, I see that the windows are barred, that the door is strongly bound. In short, this well-masked edifice is the Convent jail; and it flashes on me quickly that behind these grated frames, against which the doves are pecking and cooing, lies the mystery of Solovetsk.

In going next day round the Convent-yards and walls, with my two attending Fathers, dropping into the quass-house, the school, the dyeing-room, the tan-yard, and the Weavers' tower, I lead the way, as if by merest chance, into this pigeons' court. Referring to the Archimandrite's tale of the doves, I ask to have that story told again. Hundreds of birds are cooing and crying on the window-sills, just as they may have done on the eventful feast of Our Lady of Kazan. "How pretty these doves! What a song they sing!"

"Pigeons have a good place in the Convent," says the Father at my side. "You see we never touch them; doves being sacred in our eyes on account of that scene on the Jordan, when the Holy Ghost came down to our Lord in the form of a dove."

"They seem to build by preference in this court."

"Yes, it is a quiet corner; no one comes into this yard; yon windows are never opened from within."

"Ah! this is the Convent prison?"

"Yes; this is the old monastic prison."

"Are any of the Fathers now confined in the place?"

"Not one. We have no criminals at Solovetsk."

"But some of the Fathers are in durance, eh? For instance, where is that monk whom we brought over from Archangel in disgrace? Is he not here?"

"No; he has been sent to the Desert near Striking Hill."

"Is that considered much of a penalty?"

"By men like him, it is. In the Desert he will be alone; will see no women, and get no drink. In twelve months he will come back to the Convent another man."

"Let us go up into this prison and see the empty cells."

"Not now."

"Why not? I am curious about old prisons; especially about church prisons; and can tell you how the dungeons of Solovetsk would look beside those of Seville, Antwerp, and Rome."

"We cannot enter; it is not allowed."

"Not allowed to see empty cells! Were you not told to show me every part of the Convent? Is there a place into which visitors must not come?"

The two Fathers step aside for a private talk, during which I feed the pigeons and hum a tune.

"We cannot go in there,—at least, to-day."

"Good!" I answer, in a careless tone; "get leave, and we will come this way to-morrow. . . . . Stay! To-morrow we sail to Zaet. Why not go in at once and finish what we have yet to see down here?"

They feel that time would be gained by going

in now; but then, they have no keys. All keys are kept in the guard-room, under the lieutenant's eyes. More talk takes place between the monks; and doubt on doubt arises as to the limit of their powers. Their visitor hums a tune, and throws more crumbs of bread among the doves, who frisk and flutter to his feet, until the windows are left quite bare. A Father passes into a house; is absent some time; returns with an officer in uniform carrying keys. While they are mounting steps, and opening doors, the pilgrim goes on feeding doves, as though he did not care one whit to follow and see the cells. But when the doors roll back on their rusty hinges, he carelessly follows his guides up the prison steps.

The first floor consists of a long dark corridor, underground; ten or twelve vaults arranged in a double row. These cells are dark and empty. The visitor enters them one by one, pokes the wall with his stick, and strikes a light in each, to be sure that no one lies there unobserved; telling the officer and the monks long yarns about underground vaults and wells in Antwerp, Rome, and Seville. Climbing the stairs to an upper floor, he finds a sentinel on duty pacing a strong ante-room; and feels that here, at least, some prisoner must be kept under watch and ward. An iron-bound door is now unlocked, and the visitor passes with his guides into an empty corridor with cells on either side; corresponding in size and number with the vaults below. Every door in that corridor save one is open. That one door is closed and barred.

"Some one in there?"

"No one?" says the Father; but in a puzzled tone of voice, and looking at the officer with inquiring eyes.

"Well, yes; a prisoner," says that personage.

"Let us go in. Open the door."

Looking at the monks, and seeing no sign of opposition on their part, the soldier turns the key; and as we push the door back on its rusty hinge, a young man, tall and soldier-like, with long black beard, and curious eyes, springs up from a pallet; and snatching a coverlet, wraps the loose garment round his all but naked limbs.

"What is your name?" the visitor asks; going in at once, and taking him by the hand.

"Pushkin," he answers softly; "Adrian Pushkin."

"How long have you been confined at Solovetsk?"

"Three years; about three years."

"For what offence?"

He stares in wonder, with a wandering light in his eye that tells his secret in a flash.

"Have you been tried by any court?"

The officer interferes; the sentinel on guard is called; and we are huddled by the soldiers,—doing what they are told –from the prisoner's cell.

"What has he done?" I ask the Fathers, when the door is slammed upon the captive's face.

"We do not know, except in part. He is condemned by the Holy Governing Synod. He denies our Lord." More than this could not be learned.

"A mad young man," sighs the monk; "he

might have gone home long ago; but he would not send for a pope, and kiss the cross. He is now of better mind; if one can say he has any mind. A mad young man!"

There is yet another flight of steps. "Let us go up and see the whole."

We climb the stair, and find a second sentinel in the second ante-room. More prisoners then, in this upper ward! The door which leads into the corridor being opened, the visitor sees that here again the cells are empty,—and the doors a-jar—in every case but one. A door is locked; and in the cell behind that door they say an old man lodges; a prisoner in the Convent for many years.

"How long?"

"One hardly knows," replies the monk: "he was here when most of us came to Solovetsk. He is an obstinate fellow; quiet in his ways; but full of talk; he worries you to death; and you can teach him nothing. More than one of our Archimandrites, having pity on his case, has striven to lead him into a better path. An evil spirit is in his soul."

"Who is he?"

"A man of rank; in his youth an officer in the army."

"Then you know his name?"

"We never talk of him; it is against the rules. We pray for him, and such as he is; and he needs our prayers. A bad Russian, a bad Christian, he denies our holy Church."

"Does he ever go out?"

"In winter, yes; in summer, no. He might go to mass; but he refuses to accept the boon. He says we do not worship God aright; he thinks himself wiser than the Holy Governing Synod—he! But in winter days, when the pilgrims have gone away, he is allowed to walk on the rampart wall, attended by a sentinel to prevent his flight."

"Has he ever attempted flight?"

"Attempted! Yes; he got away from the Convent; crossed the sea; went inland, and we lost him. If he could have held his peace, he might have been free to this very hour; but he could not hold his tongue; and then he was captured and brought back."

"Where was he taken?"

"No one knows. He came back pale and worn. Since then he has been guarded with greater care."

Here, then, is the prisoner whom I wish to see; the spectre of the wall; the figure taken for the prince; the man in whom centres so many hopes. "Open the door!" My tone compels them either to obey at once or go for orders to the Archimandrite's house. A parley of the officer and monks takes place; ending, after much ado, in the door being unlocked (to save them trouble), and the whole party passing into the prisoner's cell.

An aged, handsome man, like Kossuth in appearance, starts astonished from his seat; unused, as it would seem, to such disturbance of his cell. A small table, a few books, a pallet bed, are the only furnishings of his room, the window of which is ribbed and crossed with iron, and the sill bespattered with dirt of doves. A table holds some scraps of books and journals; the prisoner being allowed, it seems, to receive such things from the outer world, though he is not permitted to send out a single line of writing. Pencils and pens are banished from his cell. Tall, upright, spare; with the bearing of a soldier and a gentleman; he wraps his cloak round his shoulder, and comes forward to meet his unexpected guests. The monks present me in form as a stranger visiting Solovetsk, without mentioning *his* name to me. He holds out his hand and smiles; receiving me with the grace of a gentleman offering the courtesies of his house. A man of noble presence and courtly bearing; *not*, however, the Grand Duke Constantine, as fishermen and pilgrims say!

"Your name is?"

"Ilyin; Nicolas Ilyin."

"You have been here long?"

Shaking his head in a feeble way, he mutters to himself, as it were, like one who is trying to recall a dream. I put the question again; this time in German. Then he faintly smiles; a big tear starting in his eye. "Excuse me, Sir," he sighs, "I have forgotten most things; even the use of speech. Once I spoke French easily. Now I have all but forgotten my mother tongue."

"You have been here for years?"

"Yes; many. I wait upon the Lord. In His own time my prayer will be heard, and my deliverance come."

"You must not speak with this prisoner," says

the officer on duty; "no one is allowed to speak with him." The lieutenant is not uncivil; but he stands in a place of trust; and has to think of duty to his colonel before he can dream of courtesy to his guest.

In a moment we are in the Pigeons' court. The iron gates are locked; the birds are fluttering on the sills; and the prisoners are alone once more.

CHAPTER XXII.

Nicolas Ilyin.

Leaving Solovetsk for the South, I keep the figure of this aged prisoner in my mind, and by asking questions here and there, acquire in time a general notion of his course of life. But much of it remains dark to me, until, on my return from Kertch and Kief to St. Petersburg, the means are found for me of opening up a secret source.

The details now to be given from this secret source—controlled by other and independent facts—will throw a flood of light into some of the darkest corners of Russian life, and bring to the front some part of the obstacles through which a reforming Emperor has to march.

It will be also seen that in the story of Ilyin's career, there are points—apart from what relates to the Convent Spectre, and the likeness to Constantine the First—which might account for some of the sympathy shown for him by Poles.

Ilyin seems to have been born in Poland; his mother was certainly a Pole. His father, though of Swedish origin, held the rank of General in the imperial service. At an early age the boy was sent by General Ilyin to the Jesuits' College in Polotsk; that famous school in which, according to report, so many young men of family were led astray in the opening years of Alexander the First. The names he bore inclined him to devote his mind to sacred studies. Nicolas is the poor man's saint, and Ilyin is the Russian form of Elias, the Hebrew Prophet. It is not by chance, he thought, that men inherit and receive such names.

He was highly trained. In the schoolroom he was noted for his gentle ways, his studious habits, his religious turn of mind. He neither drank nor swore; he neither danced nor gamed. When the time arrived for him to leave his college and join the army, he passed a good examination, took a high degree, and entered an artillery corps with the rank of ensign. By his new comrades he was noted for his power of work, for his scorn of pleasure, for his purity of life. A hard reader, he gave up his nights and days to studies which were then unusual in the mess-room and the camp. While other young men were drinking deep and dancing late in their garrison-towns, he was giving up the hours that could be snatched from drill and gunnery, to Newton on the Apocalypse, to Swedenborg on Heaven and Hell, to Bengel on the Number of the Beast. What his religious doctrines were in these early days, we can only guess. His father seems to have been a Greek Catholic, his mother a Roman Catholic; and we know too much of the genius which inspired the Jesuits' College in Polotsk to doubt that every effort would be made by the Fathers to win such a student as Nicolas Ilyin to their side.

In Polotsk, as in nearly all Polish towns, reside a good many learned Jews. Led by his Apocalyptic studies to seek the acquaintance of Rabbins, Ilyin talked with these new friends about his studies, and even went with them to their synagogue; in the ritual of which he found a world of mystical meaning not suspected by the Jews themselves. In conning the Mishna and Gemara, he began to dream that a confession of faith, a form of prayer, a mode of communion, might be framed, by help of God's Holy Spirit, which would place the great family of Abraham under a common flag. A dream, it may be, yet a noble dream!

Ilyin toyed with this idea, until he fancied that the time for a reconciliation of all the religious societies owning the God of Abraham for their father was close at hand; and that he, Nicolas Ilyin —born of a Greek father and a Catholic mother; bearing the names of a Hebrew Prophet and a Russian Saint; instructed, first by Jesuits and then by Rabbins; serving in the armies of an Orthodox Emperor—was the chosen prophet of this reign of grace and peace. A Vision helped him to accept his mission, and to form his plan.

Taking the Hebrew creed, not only as more ancient and venerable, but as simpler in form than any rival, he made it the foundation for a wide and comprehensive church. Beginning with God, he closed with man. Setting aside, as things indifferent, all the points on which men disagree, he got rid of the immaculate conception, the symbol of the cross, the form of baptism, the practice of confession, the official Church, and the sacerdotal caste. In his broad review, nothing was of first importance save the Unity of God, the Fraternity of Men.

Gifted with a noble presence and an eloquent tongue, he began to teach this doctrine of the coming time; announcing his belief in a general reconciliation of all the Friends of God. The monks who have lodged him in the Frozen Sea, accuse him of deceit; alleging that he affected zeal for the Orthodox faith; and that on converting General Vronbel, his superior officer, from the Roman church to the Russian church, he sought, as a reward for this service, a license to go about and preach. The facts may be truly stated; yet the moral may be falsely drawn. A general in the Russian service, not of the national creed, has very few means of satisfying his spiritual wants. Unless he is serving in some great city, a Roman Catholic can no more go to mass, than a Lutheran can go to sermon; and an officer of either confession is apt to smoke a pipe and play at cards, while his Orthodox troops are attending mass. Ilyin may have deemed it better for Vronbel to become a good Greek, than remain a bad Catholic. In these early days of his religious strife, he seems to have dreamt that the Orthodox Church afforded him the readiest means of reconciling creeds and men. In bringing strangers into that fold, he was putting them into the better way. Anyhow, he converted his general, and obtained from his bishop the right to preach.

It was the hope of his bishop that he would bring in stragglers to the fold; not that he should set up for himself a broader camp in another name and under a bolder flag. Ilyin went out among the sectaries who abound in every province of the empire; and to these men of wayward mind he preached a doctrine which his ecclesiastical patrons fancied to be that of the Orthodox faith. In every place he drew to himself the hearts of men; winning them alike by the splendour of his eloquence and by the purity of his life.

Early married, early blessed with children, happy in his home, Ilyin could give up hand and heart to the work he had found. He took from the Book of Revelation, the name of Right Hand Brethren, as an appropriate title for all true members of the church; his purpose being to proclaim the present unity and future salvation of all the Friends of God.

A good soldier, a good man of business, Ilyin was sent to the government works, in the province of Perm, in the Ural Mountains, where he found time in the midst of his purely military duties, for preaching among the poor, and drawing some of those who had strayed into separation back into the Orthodox fold. His enemies admit that in those days of his work in the Ural Mountains he lived a holy life. Going on state affairs to the mines of Barancha, where the government owns a great many iron works and steel works, he saw among the sectaries of that district, most of whom were exiles suffering for their conscience sake, a field for the exercise of his talents as a preacher of the word, a reconciler of men. But the martyrs of free thought whom he met in the mines of Barancha, were to him what the Kaffir chieftains were to the Bishop of Natal. They put him to the test. They showed him the darker side of his cause. They led him to doubt whether reconciliation was to be expected from metropolites and monks. Forced into a sharper scrutiny of his own belief, Ilyin at length gave up his advocacy of the Orthodox faith, and even ceased to attend the Orthodox mass.

A secret church was slowly formed in the province of Perm, of which Ilyin was the chief. Not much was known in high quarters about his doings, until Protopopoff, one of his pupils, was accused of some trifling offence, connected with the public service, and brought to trial. Protopopoff was a leading man among the Ural dissenters. His true offence was some expression against the church. Ilyin appeared in public as his friend and advocate. Protopopoff was condemned; and Ilyin closely watched. Ere long, the Director General of the Ural Mines reported to his chief, the Minister of Finance in St. Petersburg, that in one of his districts he had found existing among the miners a new religious body, calling themselves—in secret— Right-hand Brethren, of which body, Nicolas Ilyin, Captain of Artillery in the Emperor's service, was the chief and priest.

Not a little frightened by his discoveries, the Director General lost his head. In his report to the Minister of Finance, he said a good deal of these Reconcilers that was not true. He charged them with circumcising children, with advocating a community of goods and lands, with propagating doctrines fatally at war with imperial order in Church and State.

It is true that under the name of Gospel Love, the followers of Ilyin taught very strongly the necessity and sanctity of mutual help. They spoke to the poor, and bade them take heart of grace; bidding them look, not only for bliss in a better world, but for a reign of peace and plenty on the earth. In the great questions of serf and soil, two points around which all popular politics then moved, they took a part with the peasant against his lord, though Ilyin was himself of noble birth. These things appeared to the Director General of Mines anarchical and dangerous, and Ilyin was denounced by him to the Minister of Finance as a man who was compromising the public peace.

But the fact which more than all else struck the Council in St. Petersburg, was the zeal of Ilyin's pupils in spreading his doctrine of the unity and brotherhood of mankind. The new society was said to be perfect in unity. The first article of their association was the need for missionary work; and every member of the sect was an apostle, eager to spend his strength and give his life in building up the Friends of God. A man who either could not or would not convert the gentile was considered unworthy of a place on His Right Hand. At the end of seven years a man who brought no sheep into the fold was expelled as wanting in holy fire. Ilyin is alleged to have declared that there was no salvation beyond the pale of this new church, and that all those who professed any other creed would find their position at the Last Day on the left hand of God, while the true Brethren found their seats on His right. This story is not likely to be true; and an intolerant church is always ready with such a cry. It is not asserted that the new church had any printed books or even circulars, in which these things were taught. The doctrine was alleged to be contained in certain manuscript gospels, copied by proselytes and passed from one member to another; such manuscript gospels having been written, in the first instance at least, by Ilyin himself.

A special commission was named by the Ministers to investigate the facts; and this commission, proceeding at once into the Ural mines, arrested many of the members, and seized some specimens of these fugitive gospel sheets. Ilyin, questioned by the commissioners, avowed himself the author of these Gospel tracts, which, he showed them, were chiefly copies of sayings extracted from the Sermon on the Mount. In scathing terms, he challenged the right of these commissioners to judge and condemn the words of Christ. Struck by his eloquence and courage, the commission hardly knew what to say; but as practical men, they hinted that a captain of the imperial artillery, holding such doctrines, must be unsound in mind.

A report from these commissioners being sent, as usual, to the Holy Governing Synod, that board of monks made very short work of this pretender to sacred gifts. The Reconciler of creeds and men was lodged in the Convent of the Frozen Sea, until he should put away his tolerance, give up his dream of reconciliation, and submit his conscience to the guidance of a monk.

And so the Reconciler rests in his Convent ward. The Holy Governing Synod treats such men as children who have gone astray; looking forward to the wanderer coming round to his former state. The sentence, therefore, runs in some such form as this: "You will be sent to . . . where you will stay, under sound discipline, until you have been brought to a better mind." Unless the man is a rogue, and yields in policy, one sees how long such sentences are likely to endure!

Nicolas Ilyin is a learned man, with whom no monk in the Convent of Solovetsk is able to contend in speech. A former Archimandrite tried his skill; but the prisoner's verbal fence and knowledge of scripture were too much for his feeble powers; and the man who had repulsed the English fleet retired discomfited from Ilyin's cell.

Once the prisoner got away, by help of soldiers who had known him in his happier days. Escaping in a boat to Onega Point, he might have gone his way overland, protected by the people; but instead of hiding himself from his pursuers, he began to teach and preach. Denounced by the police, he was quickly sent back to his dungeon; while the soldiers who had borne some share in his escape were sent to the Siberian mines for life.

The noble name and courtly family of Ilyin are supposed to have saved the arrested fugitive from convict labour in the mines.

My efforts to procure a pardon for the old man failed; at least, for a time; the answer to my plea being sent to me in these vague words:—"Après l'examen du dossier de l'affaire d'Ilyin, il resulte qu'il n'y a pas eu d'arrêt de mise en liberté." Yet men like Nicolas Ilyin are the salt of this earth men who will go through fire and water for their; thought; men who would live a true life in a dungeon rather than a false life in the richest mansions of the world!

CHAPTER XXIII.

Adrian Pushkin.

EXCEPT the fact of their having been lodged in the Convent of Solovetsk, in neighbouring cells, under the same hard rule, Adrian Pushkin and Nicolas Ilyin have nothing in common; neither age nor rank; neither learning nor talent; not an opinion; not a sympathy; not a purpose. Pushkin is young, Ilyin is old. Pushkin is of burgher, Ilyin of noble birth. Pushkin is uneducated in the higher sense; Ilyin is a scholar to whom all systems of philosophy lie open. Pushkin is not clever; Ilyin is considered, even by his persecutors, as a man of the highest powers.

Yet Pushkin's story, from the man's obscurity, affords a still more curious instance of the dark and difficult way through which a beneficent and reforming government has to pass.

Early in the spring of 1866, a youth of good repute in his class and district, that of a small burgher, in the town of Perm, began to make a stir on the Ural slopes, by announcing to the peasant dissenters of that region the second coming of our Lord, and offering himself as the reigning Christ!

Such an event is too common to excite remark in the upper ranks, until it has been seen by trial whether the announcement takes much hold on the peasant mind. In Pushkin's case, the neighbours knew their prophet well. From his cradle he had been frail in body and flushed in mind. When he was twenty years old, the doctors were consulted on his state of mind; and though they would not then pronounce him crazy, they reported him as a youth of weak and febrile pulse, afflicted with disease of the heart; a boy who might at any moment of his life go mad. Easy work, in country air, was recommended. A place was got for him in the country, on the Countess Strogonof's estate, not far from Perm. He was made a kind of clerk and overseer; a place of trust, in which the work was light; but even this light labour proved too great for him to bear. In doing his duty to his mistress, his mind gave way; and when the light went out on earth, the poor idiot offered his help in leading other men up to heaven.

Many of the people near him knew that he was crazed; but his unsettled wits were rather a help than hindrance to his success in stirring up the village wine-shop and the workman's shed. In every part of the East some touch of idiotcy is looked for in a holy man; the wandering eye, the broken phrase, the distracted mien, being read as signs of the Holy Spirit. The province of Perm is rich in sectaries; many of whom watch and pray continually for the second coming of our Lord. Among these sectaries, Adrian found some listeners to his tale. He spoke to the poor, and of the poor. Calling the peasants to his side, he pictured to them a kingdom of heaven in which they would owe no taxes and pay no rent. The earth, he told them, was the Lord's; a paradise given by Him as a possession to His saints. What peasant would not hear such news with joy? A gospel preached in the village wine-shop and the workman's shed, was soon made known by its fruits; and the Governor of Perm was told that tenants were refusing to pay their rent and to render service, on the ground that the kingdom of heaven was come and that Christ had begun to reign.

Adrian was now arrested, and being placed before the Secret Consultative Committee of Perm, he was found guilty of having preached false doctrine and advocated unsocial measures; of having taught that the taxes were heavy, that the peasants should possess the land, that dues and service ought to be refused. Knowing that the young man was mad, the Secret Consultative Committee saw that they could never treat his case like that of a man in perfect health of body and mind. They thought the Governor of Perm might request the Holy Governing Synod to consent that Pushkin should be simply lodged in some country convent, where he might live in peace, and, under gentle treatment, hope to regain his wandering sense.

But the Holy Governing Synod pays scant heed to lay opinion. Judging the young man's fault with sharper anger than the Secret Consultative Committee of Perm had done, they sent him to Solovetsk; not until he should recover his sense and could resume his duties as a clerk, but until such time as he should recant his doctrines and publicly return to the Orthodox fold.

Valouef, Minister of the Interior, received from Perm a copy of this synodal resolution, which he saw, as a layman, that he could not carry out, except by flying in the face of Russian law. The man was mad. The Holy Governing Synod treated him as sane. But how could he, a jurist, cast a man into prison for being of unsound mind? No code in the world would sanction such a course; no court in Russia would sustain him in such an act. Of course, the Holy Governing Synod was a light unto itself; but here the civil power was asked to take a part which in the Minister's conscience was against the spirit and letter of the imperial code.

It was a case of peril on either side. Such things had been done so often in former years, that the Church expected them to go on for ever; and the monks were certain to resist, to slander, and destroy the man who should come between them and their prey. Valouef, acting with prudence, brought the report before a Council of Ministers, and, after much debate, not only of the special facts but of the guiding rules, the Council of Ministers agreed upon these two points:—first, that such a man as Pushkin could not be safely left at large in Perm; second, that it would be against the whole spirit of Russian law to punish a man for being out of his mind.

On these two principles being adopted, Valouef was recommended by the Council of Ministers to procure the Emperor's leave for Adrian Pushkin to be brought from Perm to St. Petersburg, for the purpose of undergoing other and more searching medical tests. Carrying his minute-book to the Emperor, Valouef explained the facts, together with the rules laid down, and His Majesty, adopting the suggestion, wrote with his own hand these words across the page:—"Let this be done according to the Minister of the Interior's advice. Oct. 21, 1866."

On this humane order, Pushkin was brought from Perm to St. Petersburg, where he was placed before a board of medical men. After much care and thought had been given to the subject, this medical board declared that Pushkin was unsound of brain, and could not be held responsible for his words and acts.

So far then as Emperor and ministers could go, the course of justice was smooth and straight; but then came up the question of what the Church would say. A board of monks had ordered Pushkin to be lodged in the dungeons of Solovetsk until he repented of his sins. A board of medical men had found him out of his mind; and a council of ministers, acting on their report, had come to the conclusion that, according to law, he could not be lodged in jail. His Majesty was become a party to the course of secular justice by having signed, with his own hand, the order for Adrian to be fetched from Perm and subjected to a higher class of medical tests. Emperor, ministers, physicians, stood on one side; on the other side stood a board of monks. Which was to have their way?

The Holy Governing Synod held their ground;

and in a question of false teaching it was impossible to oppose their vote. They knew, as well as the doctors, that Adrian was insane; but then, they said, all heretics are more or less insane. The malady of unbelief is not a thing for men of science to understand. They, and not a medical board, could purge a sufferer like Pushkin of his evil spirit. They said he must be sent, as ordered, to the Frozen Sea.

No minister could sign the warrant for his removal after what had passed; and powerful as they are, the Holy Governing Synod have to use the civil arm. The dead-lock was complete. But here came into play the silent and inscrutable agency of the secret police. These secret police have a life apart from that of every other body in the State. They think for every one; they act for every one. So long as law is clear and justice prompt, they may be silent—looking on; but when the hour of conflict comes, when great tribunals are at feud, when no one else can see their way, these officers step to the front, set aside codes and rules, precedents and decisions, as so much idle stuff, assume a right to judge the judges, to replace the ministers, and, in the name of public safety, do what they consider, in their wisdom, best for all.

The men who form this secret body are not called police, but "members of the third section of his imperial Majesty's chancellery." They are highly conservative, not to say despotic, in their views; and said to feel a particular joy when thwarting men of science and overruling judgments given in the courts of law. One general rule defines the power which they can bring to bear in such a case as that of Adrian Pushkin. If justice seems to them to have failed, and they are firmly persuaded—they must be "firmly persuaded"—that the public service requires "exclusive measures" to be adopted, they are free to act.

On the whole, these secret agents side with power against law, with usage against reform, with all that is old against everything that is new. In Pushkin's case they sided with the monks. Over-riding Emperor, minister, council, medical board, they carried Pushkin to the White Sea, where he was placed by the Archimandrite, not in a monastic cell, but in the dismal corridor in which I found him. He is perfectly submissive, and clearly mad. He goes to mass without ado, says his prayers, confesses his sins, and seems to have returned into the arms of the official Church. The monks in charge of him have told their chiefs that he is now of right mind with regard to the true faith; and the Governor of Archangel has written to advise that he should be allowed to go back to his friends in Perm.

It is hard, however, for a man to get away from Solovetsk. A year ago, General Timashef, who has now replaced Valouef in the Ministry of the Interior, wrote to ask whether the Holy Governing Synod had not heard from the Archimandrite of Solovetsk in favour of the prisoner; and whether the time had not come for him to be given up to his friends. No answer to that letter has been received to the present day (Dec. 1869). The board of monks are slow to undo their work; the dissidents in Perm are gaining ground; and this poor madman remains a prisoner in the pigeons' yard!

CHAPTER XXIV.

Dissent.

These dissidents, who ruffle so much the patient faces of the monks, are gaining ground in other provinces of the empire as well as Perm.

Such tales as those of Ilyin and Pushkin open a passage, as it were, beneath an observer's feet; going down into crypts and chambers below the visible edifice of the Orthodox Church and Government; showing that, in the secret depths of Russian life there may be other contentions than those which are arming the married clergy against the monks. On prying into these crypts and chambers, we find a hundred points on which some part of the people differ from their Official Church.

The Emperor Nicolas would not hear of any one falling from his Church; "autocracy and orthodoxy" was his motto; and what the master would not deign to hear, the Minister of Education tried his utmost not to see. That millions of Mussulmans, Jews, and Buddhists lived beneath his sceptre, Nicolas was fond of saying; but for a countryman of his own to differ in opinion from himself was like a mutiny in his camp. The Church had fixed the belief of one and all; the only terms on which they could be saved from hell. Had *he* not sworn to observe those terms? While Nicolas lived it was silently assumed in the Winter Palace that the dissenting bodies were all put down. One Christian church existed in his empire; and never, perhaps, until his dying hour did Nicolas learn the truth about those men whom the breath of his anger was supposed to have swept away!

Outside the Winter Palace and the Official Church dissent was growing and thriving throughout his reign. No doubt some few conformed—with halters round their throats. When autocrat and monk combined to crush all those who held aloof from the state religion, the sincere dissenter had to pass through bitter times; but spiritual passion is not calmed by firing volleys into the house of prayer; and the result of thirty years of savage persecution is, that these non-conformists are to-day more numerous, wealthy, concentrated, than they were on the day when Nicolas began his reign.

No man in Russia pretends to know the names, the numbers, and the tenets of these sects, still less the secrets of their growth. A mystery is made of them on every side. The Minister of Police divides them into four large groups, which he names and classifies as follows:—

I.—DUKHOBORTSI, Champions of the Holy Spirit.
II.—MOLOKANI, Milk Drinkers.
III.—KHLYSTI, Flagellants.
IV.—SKOPTSI, Eunuchs.

In our day it is rare to find self-deception carried to so high a point as in this official list. Four groups! Why, the Russian dissenters boast, like their Hindoo brethren, of a Hundred Sects. The classification is no less strange. The Champions of the Holy Spirit are neither an ancient nor a strong society. The Milk Drinkers are of later times than the Flagellants and the Eunuchs. The Flagellants are not so numerous as the Eunuchs, though they probably surpass in strength the Champions of the Holy Spirit.

The Flagellants and Eunuchs are of ancient date,—no one knows how ancient; the Flagellants going back to the fourteenth century at least; the Eunuchs going back to the Scythian ages; while the Milk Drinkers and the Champions of the Holy Spirit sprang into life in the times of Peter the Great.

Champions of the Holy Spirit.

Though standing first in the official list, the Champions of the Holy Spirit are one of the less important sects. They write nothing, and never preach. The only book which contains their doctrine, is "The Dukhobortsi," written by a satirist and a foe! Novitski, a professor in the University of Kief, having heard of these Champions from time to time, threw what he learned about them into a squib of some eighty pages; meaning to laugh at them, and do his worst to injure them, according to his lights. His tract was offered for twenty kopeks, but no one seemed disposed to buy, until the Champions took it up, read it in simple faith, and sent a deputation to thank the professor for his service to their cause! Novitski was amused by their gravity; especially when they told him a fact of which he was not aware; that the articles of their creed had never until then been gathered into a connected group! Of this droll deputation the police got hints. Novitski, being an officer of state, was, of course, orthodox; and his book bore every sign of having been written to expose and deride the non-conforming sect. Yet the police, on hearing of that deputation, began to fear there was something wrong; and in the hope of setting things right, they put his tract on their prohibited list of books. What more could an author ask? On finding the work condemned by the police, the Champions sent to the writer, paying him many compliments and buying up every copy of his tract at fifty rubles each. Novitski made a fortune by his squib; and now, in spite of his jokes, the laughing Professor of Kief is held to be the great expounder of their creed!

The Champions build no churches and they read no Scriptures; holding, like some of our Puritan sects, that a church is but a house of logs and stones, while the temple of God is the living heart; that books are only words, deceitful words, while the conscience of man must be led and ruled by the inner light. They show a tendency towards the most ancient form of worship; holding that every father of a family is a priest. Many of them join the Jews, and undergo the rite of circumcision. Now and then they buy a copy of the Hebrew Bible, though they cannot read one word of the sacred text. They keep it in their houses as a charm.

Milk Drinkers.

The Milk Drinkers are of more importance than these Champions of the Holy Spirit.

Critics dispute the meaning of Molokani. The original seats of the Milk Drinkers are certain villages in the south country, lying on the banks of a river called the Molotchnaya, Milky stream; a river flowing past the city of Melitopol into the Sea of Azof, through a district rich in saltpetre, and pushing its waters into the sea as white as milk. But some of the sectaries whom I meet at Volsk, on the lower Volga, tell me this resemblance of name is an accident, no more. According to my local guides, the term Milk Drinker, like that of Shaker, Mormon, and, indeed, of Christian, is a term of contempt applied to them by their enemies, because they decline to keep the ordinary fasts in Lent. Milk—and what comes of milk; butter, whey, and cheese—are staples of food in every house; and a sinner who breaks his fast in Lent is pretty sure to break it on one of the articles derived from milk; chiefly by frying his potato in a pat of butter instead of in a drop of vegetable oil.

These milk people deny the sanctity and the use of fasts, holding that men who have to work require good food, to be eaten in moderation all the year round; no day stinted, no day in excess. They prefer to live by the laws of nature; asking and giving a reason for everything they do. They set their faces against monks and popes. They look on Christ with reverence, as the purest Being ever born of woman; but they deny his Oneness with the Father, and treat the miraculous part of his career on earth as a tale of later times. In a word, the Milk Drinkers are Rationalists.

The name which they give themselves is Gospel Men; for they profess to stand by the Evangelists; live with exceeding purity, and base their daily lives on what they understand to be the laws laid down for all mankind in the Sermon on the Mount. Under Nicolas they were sorely harried. Sixteen thousand men and women were seized by the police; arranged in gangs; and driven with rods and thongs across the dreary steppes and yet more dreary mountain crests into the Caucasus. In that fearful day a great many of the Milk Drinkers fled across the Pruth into Turkey, where the Sultan gave them a village, called Tulcha, for their residence. Wise and tolerant Turk! These emigrants carried their virtues and their wealth into the new country, prospered in their shops and farms, and made for their protectors beyond the Danube a thousand friends in their ancient homes.

FLAGELLANTS.

The Flagellants are older in date, stronger in number, than the Champions and the Milk Drinkers. They go back to the first year of Alexie (1645); to a time of deep distress, when the heads of men were troubled with a sense of their guilty neglect of God.

One Daniel Philipitch, a peasant in the province of Kostroma, serving in the wars of his country, ran away from his flag, declared himself the Almighty, and wandered about the empire, teaching those who would listen to his voice, his doctrine in the form of three great assertions:—I. I am God, announced by the prophets; there is no other God but me. II. There is no other doctrine. III. There is nothing new.

To these three assertions were added nine precepts:—(1) Drink no wine; (2) Remain where you are, and what you are; (3) Never marry; (4) Never swear, or name the devil; (5) Attend no wedding, christening, or other feast; (6) Never steal; (7) Keep my doctrine secret; (8) Love each other, and keep my laws; (9) Believe in the Holy Spirit. Daniel roamed about the country, preaching this gospel for several years, gathering to himself disciples in many places, though his head-quarters remained at Kostroma. He was God; and his converts called themselves God's people. Daniel chose a son, one Ivan Susloff, a peasant of Vladimir; and this Ivan Susloff chose a pretty young girl as his Virgin Mother, together with twelve apostles. Flung into prison with forty of his disciples, Susloff saw the heresy spread. It ran through the empire, and it has followers at this hour in every part of Central Russia. "God's House," Daniel's residence in the village of Staroï, still remains—held in the utmost veneration by country folk.

The chief article of their faith is the last precept given by Daniel, "Believe in the Holy Ghost."

All their discipline and service is meant to weaken the flesh and strengthen the spirit; to which end they fast very often and flog each other very much.

Great numbers of these Flagellants have been sent into the Caucasus and Siberia, where many of them have been forced to serve in the armies and in the mines.

Eunuchs.

A more singular body is that of the Beliegolubi (White Doves), called by their enemies Skoptsi (Eunuchs). These people "make themselves eunuchs for the kingdom of heaven's sake," and look on Peter the Third, whom they take to be still alive, as their priest and king. They profess to lead a life of absolute purity in the Lord; spotless, they say, as the sacrificial doves! The White Doves are believed to live like anchorites; all except a few of their prophets and leading men. They drink no whisky and no wine. They think it a sin to indulge in fish; their staple food is milk, with bread and walnut oil. White, weak, and wasting, they appear in the shops and streets like ghosts. The monks admit that they are free from most of the vices which afflict mankind. It is affirmed of them that they neither game nor quarrel; that they neither lie nor steal. The sect is secret; and any profession of the faith would make a martyr of the man upon whom was found the sign of his high calling. Seeming to be what other men are, they often escape detection, not for years only, but for life; many of them filling high places in the world; their tenets unknown to those who are counted in the ranks of their nearest friends.

The White Doves have no visible church, no visible chief. Christ is their King, and heaven their church. But the reign of Christ has not yet come; nor will the Prince of Light appear until the earth is worthy to receive Him. Two or three persons, gathered in His name, may hope to find Him in the spirit; •but not until three hundred thousand saints confess His reign will He come to abide with them in visible flesh. One day, that sacred host will be complete; the old earth and the old heaven will pass away, consumed like a scroll in the fire.

So far as I can see (for the Eunuchs print no books, and frame no articles), their leading tenet, borrowed from the East, appears to be that of a recurring Incarnation of the Word. Just as a pundit of Benares teaches that Vishnu has been born into the world many times, probably many hundred times, a White Dove holds that the Messiah is for evermore being born again into' the world which He has saved. Once He came as a peasant's child in Galilee, when the soldiers and High Priests rose on Him and slew Him. Once again He came as an emperor's grandson in Russia, when the soldiers and High Priests rose on Him again and slew Him. He did not die; for how could God be killed by man? But He withdrew into the unseen, until His hour should come. Meantime, he is with His Church, though not in His majestic and potential shape, as hero, king, and God.

The White Doves have amongst them, only known to few, a living Virgin and a living Christ. These Incarnations are not Son and Mother in their mortal shapes; in fact, the Son is generally older than the Mother; and they are not of kin, except in the Holy Spirit. The present Christ exists in his lower form; holy, not royal; pure, not perfect; waiting for the ripeness of his time, when he will once again take flesh in all his majesty as God. A Virgin is chosen in the hope that when the ripeness of His time has come, He will be born again from that Virgin's side.

Alexander the First was deeply moved by what he heard of these sectaries. He went amongst them, and held much talk with their learned men. It has been imagined that he joined their church. Under Nicolas, the "Doves" were chased and seized by the police. On proof of the fact they were tied in gangs, and sent into the Caucasus, where they lived, —and live,—at the town of Maran, a post, on the road from Poti to Kutais; waiting for Peter to arrive. A second colony exists in the town of Shemakha, on the road from Tiflis to the Caspian Sea. They are said to be docile men, doing little work on scanty food, giving no trouble, and leading an innocent and sober life. At present, they are not much worried by the police; except when some discovery, like the Plotitsen case in Tambof, excites the public mind. A Dove who keeps his counsel, and refrains from trying to convert his neighbours, ..

need not live in fear. The law is against him; his faith is forbidden; he is not allowed to sing in the streets, to hold public meetings, and to bury his dead with any of his adopted rites; these ceremonies of his faith must be done in private and in secret; yet this singular body is said to be increasing fast. They are known to be rich; they are reported to be generous. A poor man is never suspected of being a Eunuch. When the love of woman dies out, from any cause, in a man's heart, it is always succeeded by the love of money; and all the bankers and goldsmiths who have made great fortunes are suspected of being Doves. In Kertch and Moscow, you will hear of vast sums in gold and silver being paid to a single convert for submitting to their rite.

The richest Doves are said to pay large sums of money to converts, on the strength of a prophecy made by one of their holy men, that so soon as three hundred thousand disciples have been gathered into his fold, the Lord will come to reign over them in person, and to give up to them all the riches of the earth.

CHAPTER XXV.
New Sects.

THESE groups, so far from ending the volume of dissent, do little more than open it up to sight. Stories of the Flagellants and the Eunuchs are like old-world tales, the sceneries of which lie in other ages and other climes. These sects exist, no doubt; but they draw the nurture of their life from a distant world; and they have little more enmity to Church and State than what descends with them from sire to son. Committees have sat upon them; laws have been framed to suit them; ministerial papers have described them. They figure in many books, and are the subjects of much song and art. In short, they are historical sects, like the Anabaptists in Germany, the Quakers in England, the Alumbradros in Spain.

But the genius of dissent is change; and every passing day gives birth to some new form of faith. As education spreads, the sectaries multiply. "I am very much puzzled," said to me a parish priest, "by what is going on. I wish to think the best; but I have never known a peasant learn to read, and think for himself, who did not fall away into dissent." The minds of men are vexed with a thousand fears, excited by a thousand hopes; every one seems listening for a voice; and every man who has the daring to announce himself, is instantly followed by an adoring crowd. These births are in the time, and of the time; apostles born of events, and creeds arising out of present needs. They have a political side as well as a religious side. Some samples of these recent growths may be described from notes collected by me in provinces of the empire far apart; dissenting bodies of a growth so recent, that society—even in Russia—has not yet heard their names.

Little Christians.

In the past year (1868) a new sect broke out in Atkarsk, in the province of Saratof and diocese of the Bishop of Tsaritzin. Sixteen persons left the Orthodox Church, without giving notice to their parish priest. They set up a new religion, and began to preach a gospel of their own devising. Saints and altar-pieces, said these dissidents, were idols. Even the bread and wine were things of an olden time. They had a call of their own to teach, to suffer, and to build a church. This call was from Christ. They obeyed the summons by going down into the Volga, dipping each other into the flood, changing their names, and holding together a solemn feast. This scene took place in winter; Ash Wednesday, February 26th, when the waters of the Volga are locked in ice; and had to be pierced with poles. From that day they have called themselves, humbly, after the Lord's name, Little Christians.

They have no priests and hardly any form of prayer. They keep no images, use no wafers, and make no sacred oil. Instead of the consecrated bread, they bake a cake, which they afterwards worship, as a special gift from God. This cake is like a penny bun in shape and size; but in the minds of these Little Christians it possesses a potent virtue and a mystic charm.

Hearing of these secessions from his flock, the Bishop of Tsaritzin wrote to Count Tolstoi, Minister of Education, who in turn despatched his orders to the district police. These orders were, that the men were to be closely watched; that no more baptisms in the ice were to be allowed; that no more cakes were to be baked of the size and shape of a penny bun. All preaching of these new tenets was to be stopped. The bishop, living on the spot, was to be consulted on every point of procedure against the sectaries. All these orders, and some others, have been carried out; the police are happy in their labour of repression; and the heresy of the Little Christians is increasing fast.

Helpers.

A few months ago, the Governor of Kherson was amused by hearing that some villagers in his province had been arrested by the police on the ground of their being a great deal too good for honest men. It was said the men who had been cast into prison, never drank, never swore, never lied, owed no money, and never confessed their sins to the parish priest. Nobody could make them out; and the police, annoyed at not being able to make them out, whipped them off their fields, threw them into prison, and laid a statement of their suspicions before the prince.

These over-good peasants were brothers, by name Ratushni, living in the hamlet of Osnova, in which they owned some land. Not far from Osnova stands a small town called Ananief, in which lived a burgher named Vonsarski, who was also marked by the police with a black line, as being a man too good for his class. Vonsarski paid his debts and kept his word; he lived with his wife in peace; and he never attended his parish church. He, too, was seized by the police and lodged in jail, until such time as he should explain himself, and the governor's pleasure could be learned.

It is surmised that the monks set the police at work; in the hope that if nothing could be proved at first against these offenders, tongues might be loosened, tattle might come out, and some sort of charge might be framed, so soon as the fact of their lying in jail was noised abroad through the Southern steppe.

Ratushni and Vonsarski were known to be clever men; to have talked with Moravian settlers in the South. They were suspected of looking with a lenient eye on the foreign style of harnessing bullocks and driving carts. They were accused of underrating the advantages of rural communes, in favour of a more equitable and religious system of mutual help. They were called the Helpers. But their chief offence appears to have been their preference for domestic worship over that of the parish priest.

The Governor of Kherson thought his duty in the matter clear; he set the prisoners free. When the Black Clergy of his province stormed upon him, as a man abetting heresy and schism, he quoted paragraph Eleven in his imperial master's Minute on the treatment of Dissent; a paragraph laying down the rule that every man is free to believe as he likes, so long as he abstains from troubling his neighbours by attempting to convert them to his creed. The Prince added a recommendation of his own, that the clergy of his province should strive in their own vocation to bring these wanderers back into the fold of God.

Non-payers of Rent.

Near Kazan, I hear of a new sect having sprung up in the province of Viatka, which is giving the Ministry much trouble. It may have been the fruit of poor Adrian Pushkin's labour (though I have not heard his name in connexion with it); the main doctrine of the Non-payers of Rent being the second article of Pushkin's creed.

The Canton of Mostovinsk, in the district of Sarapul, is the scene of this rising of poor saints against the tyrants of this world. Viatka, lying on the frontiers of Asia, with a mixed population of Russ, Finns, Bashkirs, Tartars, is one of the most curious provinces of the empire. Every sort of religion flourishes in its difficult dales; Christian, Mussulman, Buddhist, Pagan; each under scores of differing forms and names. Twenty Christian sects might be found in this single province; and as all aliens and idolaters living there have the right of being ruled by their own chiefs, it is not easy for the police to follow up all the clues of discovery on which they light. But such a body as the Non-payers of Rent could hardly conceal themselves from the public eye. If they were to live their life and obey their teachers, they must come into the open day, avow their doctrine, and defend their creed. Such was the necessary logic of their conversion, and when rents became due they refused to pay. The debt was not so much a rental, as a rent-charge on their land. Like all crown-peasants (and these reformers had been all crown-peasants) they had received their homesteads and holdings subject to a certain liquidating charge. This charge they declined to meet on religious grounds.

Alarmed by such a revolt, the Governor of Viatka wrote to St. Petersburg for orders. He was told in answer, to make inquiries; to arrest the leaders; and to watch with care for signs of trouble. Nearly two hundred Non-payers of Rent were seized by the police; parted into groups, and put under question. Some were released on the governor's recommendation; but when I left the neighbourhood, twenty-three of these Non-paying prisoners were still in jail.

They could not see the error of their creed; they would not promise to abstain from teaching it; and worst of all, they obstinately declined to bear the stipulated burthens on their land.

What is a practical statesman to do with men who say their conscience will not suffer them to pay their rent?

CHAPTER XXVI.

More New Sects.

ON my arrival in the province of Simbirsk, every one is talking of a singular people, whose proceedings have been recently brought to light. One Peter Mironoff, a private soldier in the Syzran regiment, has set up a new religion, which is to be professed in secret and to have no name. Peter is known as a good sort of man; pious, orderly, sedate; a soldier never absent from his drill; a penitent who never shirked his priest. Nothing fantastic was expected from him. It is said that he began by converting fourteen of his comrades, all of whom swore that they would hold the truth in private, that they would act so as to divert suspicion, that they would suffer exile, torture, death itself, but never reveal the gospel they had heard.

Not being a learned man, and having no respect for books, Peter rejects all rituals, derides all services, tears up all Lives of Saints. He holds that reading and writing are dangerous things, and takes tradition and a living teacher for his guides. Though waging war against icons and crosses, on which he stamps and frowns in his secret rites, he ostentatiously hangs a silver icon in his chamber, and wears a copper cross suspended from his neck. Teaching his pupils that true religion lies in a daily battle with the flesh, he urges them to fast and fast; abstaining, when they fast, from every kind of food, so as not to mock the Lord; and when they indulge the senses, to reject as luxuries unfit for children of grace, such food as meat and wine, as milk and eggs, as oil and fish. He warns young people against the sin of marriage, and he bids the married people live as though they were not; urging them to lead a life of purity and peace, even such as the angels are supposed to lead in heaven. By day and night he declares that the heart of man is full of good and evil; that the good may be encouraged, the evil discouraged; that fasting and prayer are the only means of driving out the evil spirits which enter into human flesh.

The men whom Peter has drawn into order reject all mysteries and signs; they wash themselves in quass, and then drink the slops. They live in peace with the world, they help each other to get on, and they implicitly obey a Holy Virgin whom they have chosen for themselves.

This Virgin, a peasant woman named Anicia, living in the village of Perevoz, in the province of Tambof, is their actual ruler; one who is even higher in authority than Peter Mironof himself. Anicia has been married about nineteen years. Fallen man, they say, can only have one teacher; and that one teacher must be a woman and a virgin. After Anicia they recognise the Saviour and St. Nicolas, as standing next in rank.

Their service, held in secret, with closed doors and shutters, begins and ends with songs; brisk music of the romping sort, accompanied by jumping, hopping, twirling; and a part of their worship has been borrowed from the Tartar mosques. They stand in prayer. They bow to the ground in adoration. They make no sign of the cross. Instead of crying, "Save me, pardon me, Mother Mary!" they cry, "Save me, pardon me, Mother Anicia Ivanovna!"

Like all the sectaries, these Nameless Ones reject the official empire and the official church.

A long time passed before Peter and his fellows were betrayed to the police, and now that the prophet and virgin have been seized, attempts are made to pass the matter by as a harmless joke. The government is puzzled how to act; nearly all the men and women accused of belonging to this lawless and blasphemous sect, being known through the province of Simbirsk for their sober and decent lives. The leaders are noted men, not only as church-goers, but supporters of the clergy in their struggles against the world. Every man whom the police has seized on suspicion, holds a certificate from his priest, in which his regularity in coming to confess his sins and receive the sacrament is duly set forth and signed. Nay, more, the parish priests come forward to testify in their behalf; for in a society which does not commonly regard priests with favour, the men who are now accused of irreligion have set an example of respect for God's ministers by asking them, on suitable occasions, to their homes.

Mother Anicia, arrested in her village, has been put under the severest trials; yet nothing has been found against her credit and her fame. She is forty years old. She has been married nineteen years. A medical board, appointed by the Governor, reports that she is still a virgin, and her neighbours, far and near, declare that she has lived amongst them a perfectly blameless life.

The police are not yet beaten in their game. An agent of their own has sworn to having been present in one of the sheds in which they conducted their indecent rites. Peter Mironoff, he declares, took down the ordinary icons from the wall, spat on them, cursed them, banged them on the floor, leaped on them, and ground them beneath his feet. After cursing the images, Mironoff kneaded a peculiar cake of ashes, foul water, and paste, in mockery of the sacred bread, and gave to every man in the shed a piece of this cake to eat. When they had eaten this cake, he called on them to strip, each one as naked as when he was born—garments being a sign of sin; and when they had all obeyed his words he bade them sing and pray together, in testimony against the world.

Each man, says this agent, is bound by the rules to choose for himself a bride of the spirit, with whom he must live in the utmost purity of life.

What can a reforming Minister do in such a case? A Jurist would be glad to leave such folk alone; but the Holy Governing Synod will not suffer them to be left alone. Peter and Anicia remain in jail; their case is under consideration; and the model soldier and blameless villager will probably end their days in a Siberian mine.

Counters.

In the province of Saratof, a wild steppe country, lying between the lands of the Kalmuks and the Don Kozáks, I hear of a new sect, called the Counters or Enumerators (Chislenniki). The high-priest of this congregation is one Taras Maxim, a peasant of Semenof, one of the bleak log villages in the black soil country.

Taras speaks of having been out one night in a wood when he met a venerable man holding in his hands a Book. This Book had been given to the old man by an angel, and the old man offered to let Taras read it. Parting the leaves, he found the writing in the sacred Slavonic tongue, and the words a message of salvation to all living men. The Book declared that the people of God must be counted and set apart from the world. It spoke of the official church as the devil's church. It showed that men have confused the order of time so as to profane with secular work the day originally set apart for rest; that Thursday is the seventh day, the true Sabbath, to be kept for ever holy in the name of God. It mentioned saints and angels with contempt; denounced the official fasts as works of Satan; and proclaimed in future only one fast a-year. It spoke of the seven sacraments as delusions, to be wholly banished from the Church of God. It said the priesthood was unnecessary and unlawful; every man was a priest, empowered by Heaven to confess penitents, to read the service, and inter the dead.

Having read all these things, and some others,

in the Book, Taras Maxim left his venerable host in the wood, and going back into Semenof told a friend what he had seen and learned. Men and women listened to his tale, and, being anxious for salvation, they counted themselves off from a corrupt society, and founded the Secret Semenof Church.

So far as I could learn—the sect being unlawful and the rites performed in private—one great purpose seems to inspire these Counters; that of pouring contempt in phrase and gesture on the forms of legal and official life. Sometimes, I can hardly doubt, they carry this protest to the length of indecent riot. Holding that Sunday is not a holy day, they meet in their sheds and barns on Sunday morning, while the village pope is saying mass, and having closed the door and planted watchers in the street, they sing and dance, they gibe and sneer; using, it is said, the roughest Biblical language to denounce, the coarsest Oriental methods to defile, the neighbours whom they regard as enemies of God.

Semenof stands east of Jerusalem, and even east of Mecca.

Maxim's chief theological tenet refers to sin. Man has to be saved from sin. Unless he sins, he cannot be saved. To commit sin, is therefore the first step towards redemption. Hence, it is inferred by the police that Maxim and his pupils rather smile on sinners, especially on female sinners, as persons who are likely to become the objects of peculiar grace. Outside their body, these Counters are regarded, even by liberal men, as an immoral and unsocial sect.

NAPOLEONISTS.

In Moscow, I hear of a body of worshippers who have the singular quality of drawing their hope from a foreign soil. These men are Napoleonists. Like all the dissenting sects, they hate the official empire and deride the official church. Seeing that the chief enemy of Russia in modern times was Napoleon, they take him to have been, literally, that Messiah which he assumed to be, in a certain mystical sense, to the oppressed and divided Poles; and they have raised the Corsican hero into the rank of a Slavonic god.

Their society is secret, and their worship private. That they live and thrive, as an organized society, is affirmed by those who know their country well. Their meetings are held with closed doors and windows, under the very eyes of the police; but this is the case with so many sects in Moscow, that their immunity from detection need excite no wonder in our eyes. Making a sort of altar in their room, they place on it a bust of the foreign prince, and fall on their knees before it. Busts of Napoleon are found in many houses; in none more frequently than in those of the imperial race. I have been in most of these imperial dwellings, and do not recollect one, from the Winter Palace to the Farm, in which there was not a bust of their splendid foe.

The Napoleonists say their Messiah is still alive, and in the flesh; that he escaped from the snares of his enemies; that he crossed the seas from St. Helena to Central Asia; that he dwells in Irkutsk, near Lake Baikal, on the borders of Chinese Tartary; that in his own good time he will come back to them, heal their sectional quarrels, raise a great army, and put the partizans of Satan, the reigning dynasty and acting ministers, to the sword.

CHAPTER XXVII.

The Popular Church.

THESE secret sects and parties would be curious studies—and little more—if they stood apart, and had to live or die by forces of their own. In such a case they would be hardly more important than the English Levellers and the Yankee Come-Outers; but these Russian dissidents are symptoms of a disease in the imperial body, not the disease itself. They live on the popular aversion to an Official Church.

It is not yet understood in England and America that a Popular Church exists in Russia side by side with the Official Church. It is not yet suspected in England and America that this Popular Church exists in sleepless enmity and eternal conflict with this Official Church. Yet in this fact of facts lies the key to every estimate of Russian progress and Russian power.

This Popular Church consists of the Old Believers; men who reject the pretended "reforms" of Patriarch Nikon, and follow their fathers in observing the more Ancient Rite. "You will find in our country," said to me a priest of this Ancient Faith, "a church of Byzantium, and a church of Bethlehem; a new Voice and an old Voice; a system framed by man, and a gospel given by God."

No one has ever yet counted the men who stand aloof from the State Church as Old Believers. By the government they have been sometimes treated in a vague and foolish way as dissenters; though the governments have never had the courage to count them as dissenters in the official papers. Known to be sources of weakness in the empire, they have been hated, feared, cajoled, maligned; observed by spies, arrested by police, entreated by ministers; everything but counted; for the governments have not dared to face the truths which counting these Old Believers would reveal. A wiser spirit rules to-day in the Winter Palace; and this great question—greatest of all domestic questions—is being studied under all its lights. Already it is felt in governing circles—let the monks say what they will—that nothing can be safely done in Russia unless these Old Believers like it. Every new suggestion laid before the Council of Ministers is met (I have been told) by the query—"What will the Old Believers say?"

The points to be ascertained about these Old Believers are these:—How many do they count? What doctrines do they profess? What is their present relation to the empire? What concessions would reconcile them to the country and the laws?

How many do they count?

A bishop, who has travelled much in his country, tells me they are ten or eleven millions strong. A minister of state informs me they are sixteen or seventeen millions strong. "Half the people, even now, are Old Believers," says a priest from Kem;

"more than three-fourths will be the moment we are free." My own experience leads me to think this priest is right. "I tell you what I find in going through the country," writes to me a German, who has lived in Russia for thirty years, knowing the people well, yet standing free (as a Lutheran) from their local brawls; "I find, on taking the population, man by man, that *four* persons *in five* are either Old Believers now, or would be Old Believers next week, if it were understood among them that the government left them free." This statement goes beyond my point; yet I see good reason every day to recognise the fact—so long concealed in official papers—that the Old Believers are the Russian people; while the Orthodox Believers are but a courtly, official, and monastic sect.

Nearly all the Northern peasants are Old Believers; nearly all the Don Kozaks are Old Believers; more than half the population of Nijni and Kazan are Old Believers; most of the Moscow merchants are Old Believers. Excepting princes and generals, who owe their riches to imperial favour, the wealthiest men in Russia are Old Believers. The men who are making money, the men who are rising, the captains of industry, the ministers of commerce, the giants of finance,—in one word, the men of the instant future,—are members of the Popular Church.

Driving through the streets of Moscow, day by day, admiring the noble houses in town and suburb, your eye and ear are taken by surprise at every turn. "Whose house is this?" you ask. "Morozof's." "What is he?" "Morozof! why, Sir, Morozof is the richest man in Moscow; the greatest mill-owner in Russia. Fifty thousand men are toiling in his mills. He is an Old Believer."

"Who lives here?" "Soldatenkof." "What is he?" "A great merchant; a great manufacturer; one of the most powerful men in Russia. He is an Old Believer."

"Who lives in yonder palace?"

"Miss Rokhmanof. In London you have such a lady; Miss Burdett Coutts is richer, perhaps, than Miss Rokhmanof; but not more swift to do good deeds. Her house, as you see, is big; it has thirty reception-rooms. She is an Old Believer." So you drive on from dawn to dusk. You go into the bazaar—to find Old Believers owning most of the shops; you go into the University—to find Old Believers giving most of the burses; you go into the hospitals—to find Old Believers feeding nearly all the sick. The old Russ virtues—even the old Russ vices—will be found among these Old Believers; not among the polite and enervated followers of the official form. "In Russia," said to me a judge of men, "society has a ritual of her own; a ritual for the palace, for the convent, for the camp; a gorgeous ritual, fit for emperors and princes, such as the purple born might offer to barbaric kings, not such as fishermen in Galilee would invent for fishermen on the Frozen Sea."

An Old Believer clings to the baldest forms of village worship and the simplest usages of village life. Conservative in the bad sense, as in the good, he objects to every new thing, whether it be a synod of monks, a capital on foreign soil, a cup of tea sweetened with sugar, a city lit by gas. Show him a thing unknown to his fathers in Nikon's time, and you show him a thing which he will spurn as a work of the nether fiend.

These Old Believers are as much the enemies of an official empire as they are of an official church. The test of loyalty in Russia is praying for the reigning prince as a good Emperor and a good Christian; but many of these Old Believers will not pray for the reigning prince at all. Some will pray for him as Tsar, though not as Emperor; but none will pray for him as a Christian man. They look on him as reigning by a dubious title and a doubtful right. The word Emperor, they say, means Chert—Black One; the double eagle an evil spirit; the autocracy a kingdom of Antichrist.

All this confusion in her moral and political life is traceable to the times of Nikon the Patriarch; a person hardly less important to a modern observer of Russia than the great prince who is said by Old Believers to have been his bastard son.

About the time when our own Burton and Prynne were being laid in the pillory, when Hampden and Cromwell were being stayed in the Thames, a man of middle age and sour expression landed from a boat at Solovetsk, to pray at the shrine of St. Philip, and beg an asylum from the monks. He described himself as a peasant from the Volga, his father as a field-labourer in a village near Nijni. He was a married man and his wife was still alive. In his youth, he had spent some time in a monastery, and after trying domestic life for ten years, he had persuaded his partner to become a bride of Christ. Leaving her in the Convent of St. Alexie in Moscow, he had pushed out boldly into the Frozen North.

At that time, certain hermits lived on the isle of Anzersk, where the farm now stands, in whose "desert" this stranger found a home. There he took the cowl, and the name of Nikon; but his nature was so rough that he was soon engaged in bickering with his chief as he had bickered with his wife. Eleazar, founder of the desert, desired to build a church of stone in lieu of his church of pines, and the two men set out for Moscow to collect some funds. They quarrelled on their road; they quarrelled on their return. At length, the brethren rose on the new-comer, expelled him from the desert, placed him in a canoe, with bread and water, and told him to go whither he pleased, so that he never came back. Chance threw him on shore at Ki, a rock in Onega bay; where he set up a cross, and promised to erect a chapel, if the virgin whom he served would help him to get rich.

On crossing to the mainland, he became the organiser of a band of hermits on Leather Lake (Kojeozersk) in the province of Olonetz. From Leather Lake he made his spring into power and fame; for having an occasion to see the Tsar Alexie on some business, he so impressed that very poor judge of men that in a few years he was raised to the seats of Archimandrite, Bishop, Metropolite, and Patriarch.

Combining the pride of Wolsey with the subtlety

of Cranmer, Nikon set his heart on governing the Church with a sharper rod than had been used by his faint and shadowy predecessors. A burly fellow, flushed of face, red of nose, and bleary of eye, Nikon resembled a Friesland boor much more than a Moscovite monk. He revelled in pomp and show; he swelled with vanity as he sat enthroned in his cathedral near the Tsar. Feeling a priest's delight in the splendour of the Byzantine clergy, even under Turkish rule, he sought to model his own ceremonial rites on those of the Byzantine clergy, not aware that in going back to the Lower Empire he was seeking guidance from the Greeks in their corruptest time. His earlier steps were not unwise. Sending out a body of scribes, he obtained from Mount Athos copies of the most ancient and authentic sacred books, which he caused to be translated into Slavonic and compared with the books in ordinary use; and finding that errors had crept into the text, he bade his scribes prepare for him a new edition of the Scriptures and Rituals, in which the better readings should be introduced. But here his merit ends. Nikon knew no Greek; yet when the work was done for him by others, he proceeded, with an arrogant frown on his brow, to force his version on the church. The church objected; Nikon called upon the Tsar. The priests demurred to this intrusion of the civil power; and Nikon handed the protesting clergy over to the police. Alexie lent him every aid in carrying out his scheme. Yet the opposition was strong, not only in town and village, but in the Council, in the Convent, and in the

Church. Peasants and popes were equally against the changes he proposed to make. The service-books were old and venerable; they sounded musical in every ear; their very accents seemed divine. These books had been used in their sacred offices time out of mind, and twenty generations of their fathers had by them been christened, married, and laid at rest. Why should these books be thrown aside? The writings offered in their stead were foreign books. Nikon said they were better; how could Nikon know? The Patriarch was not a critic; many persons denied that he was a learned man. Instead of trying to gain support for his innovations, he forced them on the Church. Nor was he satisfied to deal with the texts alone. He changed the old cross. He trifled with the sacraments. He brought in a new mode of benediction. He altered the stamp on consecrated bread. By order of the Tsar, who could not see the end of what he was about, the Council adopted Nikon's reforms in the church; and these new Scriptures, these new services, these new sacraments, this new cross, and this new benediction, were introduced, by order of the civil power, in every church and convent throughout the land. The Nikonian Church was recognised as an Official Church.

Most of the people and their parish clergy stood up boldly for their ancient texts, especially in the far north countries, where the court had scarcely any power over the thoughts of men. The view taken in the north appears to have been something like that of our English Puritans when judging the merits and demerits of King James's version:—they thought the new Scriptures rather too worldly in tone; over-just to high dignitaries in Church and State; less likely to promote holy living and holy dying than the old. In a word, they thought them too political in their accent and their spirit.

No convent in the empire showed a sterner will to reject these innovations than the great establishment in the Frozen Sea. When Nikon's service-books arrived at Solovetsk, the brethren threw them aside in scorn. The Archimandrite, as an officer of State, took part with the Patriarch and the Tsar; but the Fathers put their Archimandrite in a boat and carried him to Kem. Having called a council of their body, they chose two leaders; Azariah, whom they elected Caterer; and Gerontie, whom they elected Bursar. All the Kozaks in the fortress joined them; and supported from the mainland by people who shared their minds, the monks of Solovetsk maintained their armed revolt against the Nikonian Church for upwards of ten years, and only fell by treachery at last.

In Orthodox accounts of this siege the captors are represented as behaving as men should behave in war. They are said to have put to the sword only such as they took in arms; and borne the rest away from Solovetsk, to be placed in convents at a distance till they came to a better mind. But many old books, possessed by peasants round the Frozen Sea, put another face on such tales. A peasant, living in the Delta, pulled up a book from a well under his kitchen floor, and showed me a passage in red and black ink, to the effect that the whole brotherhood of resisting monks was put to the sword and perished to a man.

What the besiegers won, the nation lost. This victory clove the Church in twain, and the end of Nikon's triumph has not yet been reached.

CHAPTER XXVIII.

Old Believers.

THE new service-books and crosses were ordered to be used in every Church. The Church which used them was declared official, orthodox, and holy. Every other form of public worship was put under curse and ban.

Princes, Vladikas, generals, all made haste to pray in the form most pleasing to their Tsar. Cajoled and terrified by turns, the monks became in a few years orthodox enough; and many of the parish priests, on being much pressed by the police, marched over to the stronger side. Not all; not nearly all; for thousands of the country clergymen resisted all commands to introduce into their services these suspected books; contending that the changes wrought in the sacred texts were neither warranted by fact nor justified by law. They treated them as the daring labour of a single man. Not all of those who held out against Nikon could pretend to be scholars and critics; but neither, they alleged, was Nikon himself a scholar and a critic. When he came to Solovetsk he was an ignorant peasant, too old to learn; when he was driven from Anzersk by his outraged brethren, he was as ignorant of letters as when he came. Since that time he had led a life of travel and intrigue. If they were feeble judges he was also a feeble judge.

Clinging fast to their venerable forms, the clergy

kept their altars open to a people whom neither soldiers nor police could drive to the new matins and the new mass. Many of the burghers, most of the peasants, doggedly refused to budge from their ancient chapels, to forego their favourite texts. They were Old Believers; they were the Russian Church; Nikon was the heretic, the sectarian, the dissident; and, strong in these convictions, they set their teeth against every man who fell away from the old national rite to the new official rite.

From those evil times, the people have been parted into two hostile camps; a camp of the Ancient Faith, and a camp of the Orthodox Faith; a parting which it is no abuse of words to describe as the heaviest blow that has ever fallen upon this nation; heavier than the Polish invasion, heavier than the Tartar conquest; since it sets brother against brother, and puts their common sovereign at the head of a persecuting board of monks.

One consequence of these Old Believers being driven into relations of enmity towards the government is the weakening of Russia on every side. The church is shorn of her native strength; the civil power usurps her functions; and the man who brought these evils on her was deposed from his high rank. Nikon was hardly in his grave before the office of Patriarch was abolished; and the Church was virtually absorbed into the State. The Orthodox church became a Political church; extending her limits, and ruling her congregations by the secular arm. Imperious and intolerant, she allows no reading of the Bible, no exercise of thought, no freedom of opinion, within her pale. The Old Believers suffer in their turn; not only from the persecutions to which their "obstinacy" lays them open, but from the isolation into which they have fallen.

From the moment of their protest, down to the present time, these Old Believers have been driven, by their higher virtues, into giving an unnatural prominence to ancient habits and ancient texts. Living in an old world, they see no merit in the new. According to their earnest faith, the reign of Antichrist began with Nikon; and since the time of Nikon every word spoken in their country has been false, every act committed has been wrong.

Like a Moslem and like a Jew, an Old Believer of the severer classes may be known by sight. "An Old Believer?" says a Russian friend, as we stand in a posting-yard, watching some pilgrims eat and drink; "an Old Believer,—Yes."

"How do you read the signs?"

"Observe him; see how he puts the potatoes from him with a shrug. That is a sign. He eats no sugar with his glass of tea; that also is a sign. The chances are that he will not smoke."

"Are all these notes of an Old Believer?"

"Yes; in these Northern parts. At Moscow, Nijni, and Kazan, you will find the rule less strict —especially as to drinking and smoking—least of all strict among the Don Kozaks."

"Are the Don Kozaks Old Believers?"

"Most of them are so; some say all. But the government of Nicolas strove very hard to bring them round; and seeing that these Kozaks live under martial law, their officers could press them in a hundred ways to obey the wishes of their Tsar. Their Atamans conformed to the Emperors' creed; and many of his troopers so far yielded as to hear an official mass. Yet most of them stood out; and many a fine young fellow from the Don country went to the Caucasus rather than abandon his ancient rite. You should not trust appearances too far, even among those Don Kozaks; for it is known that in spite of all that popes and police could do, more than half the Kozaks kept their faith; and fear of pressing them too far has led, in some degree, to the more tolerant system now in vogue."

"You find some difference, then, even as regards adherence to the Ancient Rite, between the north country and the south?"

"It must be so; for in the north we live the true Russian life. We come of a good stock; we live apart from the world; and we walk in our fathers' ways. We never saw a noble in our midst; we hold to our native saints and to our genuine church."

The signs by which an Old Believer is to be distinguished from the Orthodox, are of many kinds; some domestic,— such as his way of eating and drinking; others devotional,— such as his way of making the cross and marking the consecrated bread.

An Old Believer has a strong dislike to certain articles; not because they are bad in themselves, but simply because they have come into use since Nikon's time. Thus, he eats no sugar; he drinks no wine; he repudiates whisky; he smokes no pipe.

An Old Believer of the sterner sort has come to live alone; even as a Hebrew or a Parsee lives alone. He has taken hold of the Eastern doctrine that a thing is either clean or unclean, as it may happen to have been touched by men of another creed. Hence he must live apart. He can neither break bread with a stranger, nor eat of flesh which a heretic has killed. He cannot drink from a pitcher that a stranger's lip has pressed. In his opinion false belief defiles a man in body and in soul; and when he is going on a journey, he is tortured like a Hebrew with the fear of rendering himself unclean. He carries his water-jug and cup, from which no stranger is allowed to drink. He calls upon his comrades only, since he dares not eat his brown bread, and drain his basin of milk in a stranger's house. Yet homely morals cling to these men no less than homely ways. An Old Believer is not more completely set apart from his neighbours of the Orthodox rite by his peculiar habits, than by his personal virtues. Even in the north country, where folk are sober, honest, industrious, far beyond the average Russian, these members of the Popular Church are noticeable for their probity and thrift. "If you want a good workman," said to me an English mill-owner, "take an Old Believer, especially in a flax-mill."

"Why in a flax-mill?"

"You see," replied my host, "the great enemy of flax is fire; and these men neither drink nor smoke. In their hands you are always safe."

CHAPTER XXIX.

A Family of Old Believers.

In the forest village of Kondmazaro, lives a family of Old Believers, named Afanasevitch; two brothers, who till the soil, fell pines, and manufacture tar. Their house is a pile of logs; a large place, with barn and cow-shed, and a patch of field and forest. These brothers are wealthy farmers, with manly ways, blue eyes, and gentle manners. Fedor and Michael are the brothers, and Fedor has a young and dainty wife.

The family of Afanasevitch is clerical, and the two men, Fedor and Michael, were brought up as priests. On going into their house you see the signs of their calling, and on going into their barn you see a chapel, with an altar and sacred books.

That barn was built by their grandfather, in evil days, as a chapel for his flock; and during many years, the father of these men—now gone to a better place—kept up, in the privacy of his farm, the forms of worship which had come down to him from his sire, and his sire's sire. This barn has no cupola, no cross, no bell. So far as takes the eye, it is a simple barn. Inside, it is a quaint little chapel, with screen and cross, with icon and crown. It has a regular altar, with step and desk, and the customary pair of royal gates.

The father of Fedor and Michael, following in his father's wake, appeared to the outside world a farmer and woodman, while to his faithful people he was a priest of God.

These lads assisted him in the service, while his neighbours took their turn of either dropping in to mass, or mounting guard in the lane. His altars were often stripped, his books put in a well, his pictures hidden in a loft; for the police, informed of what was going on by monkish spies, were often at his gates. At length, a brighter day is dawning on the Popular Church. A new prince is on the throne; and under the White Tsar, the congregations which keep within the rules laid down are left in peace.

"You hold a service in this church?"

"My brother holds it; not myself," says Fedor, with a sigh. "My priesthood is gone from me."

"Your priesthood gone? How can a priesthood go away? Is not the law, Once a Priest always a Priest?"

"Yes, in a regular church; but we are not now a regular church, with a sacred order and an apostolic grace. We are a village priesthood only; chosen by our neighbours to serve the Lord in our common name."

"How was your personal priesthood lost?"

"By falling into sin through love. My wife, though village born, had scruples about the form of marriage in use among our people, and begged me to indulge her weakness on that point by marrying her in the parish church. It was a proper thing for her to ask; a very hard thing for me to grant;

for law and right are here at strife, and one must take his chance of rejecting either man or God. The time is not a reign of grace, and nothing that we do is lawful in the sight of Heaven. We take no sacraments; for the apostolic priesthood has passed away. No man alive has power to bind and loose, or even to marry and to shrive."

"Still you marry?"

"Yes; outwardly, according to a form; not inwardly, according to the Spirit. Besides, the law does not admit our form; the Orthodox say we are not married, and the courts declare our children basely born. Hence, some of our women crave to be wedded as the Code directs, in the parish church, by an Orthodox priest. I could not blame poor Mary for her weakness, though she wished me to marry her in a way that would insult my kindred, harass my mother, and cause me to be removed from my office, and degraded from my rank as priest. I loved the girl, and we went to church."

Fedor stands beside me, tall and lank, with mild blue eyes, and yellow locks, a serge blouse hanging round his figure, caught at the waist by a broad red belt; his figure and face suggesting less of the meek Russ peasant, than of the fiery Northern skald. Quaint books with old bronze clasps and leather ties, are in his arms. These books he spreads before me with mysterious silence, pointing out passage after passage, written in a dashing style—partly in red letters, partly in black—in the dead Slavonic tongue. He looks a very unlikely man to have lost the world for love.

"Your marriage got you into trouble?"

"Yes, a man who marries plunges into care."

"But though you have lost your priesthood, you are not expelled from the community?"

"Not expelled in words; yet I am not received into fellowship; not having yet performed the necessary acts."

"What acts?"

"The acts of penitence. Being married, I am not allowed to pass the church-door; only to stand on the outer steps, salute the worshippers, and listen to the sacred sounds. I am expected to stand in the street, bareheaded, through the summer's sun and the winter frost; to bend my knee to every one going in; to beg his pardon of my offence; and to solicit his prayers at the throne of grace."

"How long will your time of penitence last?"

"Years,—years!" he answers sadly; "if I were rich enough to do nothing else, I could be purified in six weeks. The penance is for forty days; but forty successive days; and I have never yet found time to give up forty days, in any one season, to the cleansing of my fame. But some year I shall find them."

"How does this failure affect your wife? Is she received into the Church?"

"If you note this house of God, you will observe a part railed off behind the screen; this is the female side, and has an entrance by a separate door. No woman goes in at the principal gate. The space behind the screen is not considered as lying within the Church; and there my wife can stand during service; bending to our neighbours as they enter, asking every woman to forgive her offence, and help her in prayer with her patron saint."

"Are you considered impure?"

"Yes; until our peace is made. You see an Old Believer thinks that for most people a single life is better than a wedded life. It is the will of God, that some should marry, in order that His children shall not die off the earth. Sometimes it is the will of Satan, that hell may be replenished with fallen souls. In either case, it is a sign of our lost estate; an act to be atoned by penitence and prayer. But getting married is not the whole of our offence. We went into the world; we held communion with the heathen; and we put ourselves beyond the pale of law."

"You hold the outer world to be unclean?"

"In one sense; yes. The world has been defiled by sin. A man who goes from our village into the world — who crosses the river in order to sell his deals and buy white flour — must purify himself on coming back. He may have to cut his bread with an unclean knife, to drink his water from an unclean glass. He carries his knife and cup beneath his girdle for common use; yet he may be forced, by accident, to eat with a strange knife, to drink out of a strange mug. On his return, he has to stand at the chapel door, and beg the forgiveness of every member of the community for his sins."

"Yet you are said to differ from the Orthodox clergy only in a few points?"

"On many points. We differ on the existence of a State Church; on the Holy Governing Synod; on the number of sacraments; on the benediction; on the cross; on the service-books; on the apostolical succession; and on many more. We object to the civil power in matters of faith; object to Byzantine pomp in our worship. What we want in our Church is the old Russian homeliness and heartiness; priests who are learned and sober men; bishops who are actual fathers of their flocks."

"Show me how you give the benediction."

"Christ and His apostles gave the blessing so; the first and second finger extended; the thumb on the third finger; not as the Byzantines give it, with the thumb on the first finger. We follow the usage introduced by Christ."

"You make much of that form?"

"Much for what it proves; not much for what it is. Pardon me, and I will show you. Here is a small bronze figure of our Lord; the work good and ancient; older than Nikon, older than St. Vladimir; it is said to have come from Kherson, on the Black Sea. This figure proves our case against Nikon the Monk, who altered things without reason, only to puff himself out with pride. Our Lord, you will observe, is giving the blessing, just as our saints, from Philip to Vladimir, gave it. The Greek fathers in Bethlehem bless a pilgrim in this way now. Our form is Syrian Greek, the Orthodox form is Byzantine Greek."

"And the cross?"

"We keep the old traditions of the cross. On

every ancient spire and belfry in the land you find a true cross. Observe the spires in Moscow, Novgorod, and Kief. In places it has been removed, to make way for the Latin cross; but on many towers and steeples it remains; a lofty and silent witness for the truth."

"How do you prove that your cross is the true one? Think of it; the cross was a Roman gibbet; a thing unknown to either Jew or Greek. Are not the Latins likely to have known the shape of their own penal cross?"

"All that is true; but the Holy Cross on which our Lord expired in the flesh was not a common cross, made of two logs. We know that it was built of four different trees; cypress, cedar, palm, and olive; therefore it must have had three arms."

"You take no sacraments?"

"At present, none. We have no priests ordained to bless the bread and wine. Saved without them? Yes; in the providence of God. Men were saved before sacraments; Judas Iscariot took them and was lost. A sacrament is a good form, not a saving means."

Fedor is a type of those Old Believers who are said to be slackening at the joints, in consequence of their present freedom from persecution. He has not learned to smoke; but he sees no harm in a pipe, except so far as it might cause a brother to fail and fall. He does not care for wine; but he will toss off his glass of whisky like a genuine child of the North. Some strict ones in his village drink no tea, having doubts on their mind whether tea came into use before Nikon's reign; and nearly all his neighbours refuse to mix sugar with their food, to put pipes into their mouths, to plant potatoes in their soil. Fedor objects to sugar, as being a devil's offering, purified with blood. Whisky he thinks lawful and beneficial; St. Paul having commanded Timothy to drink a little wine—which Fedor says is a shorter name for whisky—for his stomach's sake. Fedor is willing to obey St. Paul.

Fedor is a Bible-reader. Every phrase from his lips is streaked with text, and every point in his argument backed by chapter and verse. Except in some New England homesteads, I have never heard such floods of reference and quotation in my life.

"You say your church has lost the priesthood?"

"Yes; our priests are all destroyed; the heavenly gift is lost; and we are wandering in the desert without a guide. This is our trial. Our bishops have all died off; we cannot consecrate a priest; the consecrating power is in the devil's camp."

"How can you get back this gift?"

"By miracle; in no other way. The priesthood came by miracle; by miracle it will be restored."

"In our own day?"

"No; we do not hope it. Miracles come in an age of faith. *We* are not worthy of such a sign. We have to walk in our fathers' ways; to keep our children true; and hope that they may live into that better day."

"You think the Orthodox rite will be overthrown?"

"In time. In God's own time His kingdom will

be restored; and Russia will be one people and one Church."

"What would you like the government to do?"

"We want a free Church; we want to walk with our fathers; we want our old Church discipline; we want our old books, our old rituals, our old fashions; we want to read the Bible in our native tongue."

"Are the Old Believers all of one mind about these points?"

"Ha, no! There are Old Believers and Old Believers. In the north we are pretty nearly of one mind; in the south they are divided into two bodies, if not more. The government is active in Moscow; Moscow being our ancient capital; and most of the traders in that city Old Believers. Ministers are trying to win them over to the Orthodox Church. Visit the Cemetery of the Transfiguration near Moscow; there you will see what government has done."

Let us follow Fedor's hint.

CHAPTER XXX.

Cemetery of the Transfiguration.

Four or five miles from the Holy Gate, beyond the walls of Moscow, in a populous suburb, near the edge of a pool of water, lies a field containing multitudes of graves; the graves of people who were long ago struck down by plague. This field is fenced with stakes, and part of the enclosure guarded by a wall. Within this wall stand a hospital and a convent; hospital on your left, convent on your right. A huge gateway, built of stones from older piles, and quaintly coloured in Tartar panels, opens in your front. Driving up to this gate, we send in our cards—a Councillor of State, an English friend, and myself—and are instantly admitted by the chief.

"This cemetery," says our friendly guide, "is called Preobrajenski (Transfiguration), from the village close by. In the plague time (1770) it was steppe, and people threw out their dead upon it, laying them in trenches, hardly covered with a pinch of dust. The plague growing worse and worse, the village Elder got permission from Empress Catharine to build a house on the spot, to keep the peace and fumigate the dead. That house was built among the trenches. Ten years later (1781), Elia Kovielin, a brickmaker in Moscow, built among these graves a church, a cloister, and a hospital. This Kovielin was a clever man; rich in money and in friends; living in a fine house, and having the Master of Police, with governors, generals, princes, always at his board. Catharine was not aware of his being an Old Believer; but her ministers and courtiers knew him well enough. His house was a church; the pictures in his private chapel cost him fifty thousand rubles. Kovielin *was* a rich man. The monks were afraid of him, because he had friends at Court; the priests, because he had the streets and suburbs at his back. Besides, what monk or priest could rail against a man for building a Cemetery for the dead? A very clever man! You have heard the story of his magic loaf? You have not! Then you shall hear it. Paul the First, becoming aware that this edifice of the Transfiguration was an Old Believer's church, resolved to have it taken down. Kovielin drove to St. Petersburg, and found the Emperor deaf to his pleas. Voiékof, Master of Police in Moscow, having the Emperor's orders to pull down tower and wall, rode out to the Cemetery, where he was received by Kovielin, and on going away was honoured by the present of a convent loaf. A loaf! A magic loaf! Voiékof liked that lump of bread so well, that he went home and forgot to pull the Cemetery about our ears. Folk say that loaf contained a purse— five thousand rubles coined in gold. Who knows? Elia Kovielin was a clever man!"

Our guide through the courts and chapels is not an Old Believer, but an officer of State. In 1852,

Nicolas seized the Cemetery, sequestered the funds, and threw the management into official hands. The hospital he left to the Old Believers; for this great hospital is maintained in funds by the gifts of pious men; and the Emperor saw, that if his officers seized the hospital, either his budget must be charged with a new burthen, or the sick and aged people must be thrown into the streets. He seized their church, and left them their sick and aged poor.

"Kovielin's magic loaf was not the best," says the officer in charge; "these Old Believers are always rogues. When Bonaparte was lodging at the Kremlin, they went to him with gift and speech—the gift, a dish of golden rubles; saying, they came to greet him, and acknowledge him as Tsar."

"They thought he would deliver them from the tyranny of monks and priests?"

"Yes; that was what they dreamt. Napoleon humoured them like fools, and even rode down hither to see them in their village. Kovielin was dead; *he* would not have done such things. Napoleon rode round their graves, and ate of their bread and porridge; but he could not make them out. They wanted a White Tsar; not a soldier in uniform and spurs. He went away puzzled; and when he was gone the rascals took to forging government notes."

"Odd trade to conduct in a cemetery!"

"You doubt me! Ask the police; ask any friend in Moscow; ask the Councillor."

"They were suspected," says the Councillor of

State, "and their chapel was suppressed; but these events occurred in a former reign."

"What became of their chapel? Was it pulled down?"

"No; there it stands. The chapel is a rich one; Kovielin transferred to it all those pictures from his private house which had cost him fifty thousand rubles; and many rich merchants of Moscow graced it with works of art. It has been purified since, and turned into an Orthodox Church."

"An Orthodox Church!"

"Well, yes; in a sort of way. You see, the people here about are Old Believers; warm in their faith; attached to their ancient rites. In numbers only they are strong: ten millions—fifteen millions—twenty millions; no one knows how many. Long oppressed, they have lost alike their love of country and their loyalty to the Tsar; some looking wistfully for help to the Austrian Kaiser; others again dreaming of a King of France. It is of vast political moment to recover their lost allegiance; and the ministers of Nicolas conceived a plan which has been steadily carried out. The Old Believers are to be reconciled to the empire by—what shall we say?"

"A trick?"

"Well, this is the plan. The chapel is to be declared orthodox; it is to be opened by thirty monks and a dozen priests; but the monks are to be dressed in homely calico, and the ritual to be used is that employed before Nikon's time."

"You mean me to understand that the Official

Church is willing to adopt the Ancient Rites, if she may do so with her present priests?"

"Yes; the object of the government is to prove that Custom, not Belief, divides the Ancient from the Orthodox Church."

"It is an object that compels the government to meet the Old Believers more than halfway; for to give up Nikon's ritual is to give up all the principle at stake. Has the experiment of an Orthodox priest performing the Ancient rite succeeded in bringing people to the purified church?"

"Old Believers say it has completely failed. The chapel is now divided from the hospital by a moral barrier; and outside people scorn to pass the door and fall into what they call a trap. Last year the chiefs of the asylum prayed for leave to build a new wall across this courtyard, cutting off all communication with what they call their desecrated shrine. The Home Minister saw no harm in their request; but on sending their petition to the Holy Governing Synod, he met a firm refusal of the boon. The Popular Church has nothing to expect from these mitred monks."

On passing into this "desecrated shrine," we find a sombre church, in which vespers are being chanted by a dozen monks, without a single soul to listen. Most of these monks are aged men, with long hair and beards, attired in black calico robes, and wearing the ancient Russian cowl. Each monk has a small black pillow, on which he kneels and knocks his head. Church, costume, service, every point is so arranged as to take the eye and ear as homely, old and weird,—in fact, the Ancient rite.

"Do any of the Old Believers come to see you?"

"Yes, on Sundays, many," says the chief Pope; "for on Sundays we allow them to dispute in church, and they are fond of disputing with us, phrase by phrase, and rite by rite. Five or six hundred come to us—after service—to hear us questioned by their popes. We try to show them that we all belong to one and the same church; that the difference between us lies in ceremony and not in faith."

"Have you made converts to that view?"

"In Moscow, no; in Vilna, Penza, and elsewhere, our work of conciliation is said to have been more blessed."

"Those places are a long way off."

"Yes; bread that is scattered on the waters may be found in distant parts."

When I ask in official quarters on what pretence the Emperor Nicolas seized the Popular Cemetery, the answer is—that under the guise of a cemetery the Old Believers were establishing a college of their faith; from which they were sending forth missionaries, full of Bible learning, into other provinces; and that these priests and elders were attracting crowds of men from the Orthodox Church into dissent. It was alleged that they were spreading far and fast; that the parish priests were favouring them; and that every public trouble swelled their ranks. To wit, the cholera is said to have changed a thousand Orthodox persons into Old Believers every week. If it had raged two years, the Orthodox faith would have died a natural death. For in cases of public panic the Russian people have an irresistible longing to fall back upon their ancient ways. It is the cry of Hebrews in dismay: "Your tents! back to your tents!" All Eastern nations have this homely and conservative passion in their blood.

"These were the actual reasons," says the Councillor of State; "but the cause assigned for interference was the scandal of the forged bank-notes."

"Surely no one believes that scandal?"

"Every one believes it. Only last year this scandal led to the perpetration of a curious crime."

"What sort of crime?"

"At dusk on a wintry day, when all the offices in the Cemetery were closed, a cavalcade dashed suddenly to the door. A colonel of gendarmes leapt from a drojki, followed by a master of police. Four gendarmes and four citizens of Moscow came with them. Pushing into the chief office, they asked to see the strong box, and to have it opened in their presence. As the clerk looked shy, the colonel of gendarmes was sharp and rude. They were accused, he said, of forging ruble notes, and he had come by order of the Governor-general, Prince Vladimir Dolgorouki, to open their strong box under the eyes of four eminent merchants and the master of police. He laid the Prince's mandate down; he showed his own commission; and then in an imperial tone demanded to have the keys! The keys could not be found; the treasurer was gone to Moscow, and would not return that night. "Then seal your box," said the colonel of gendarmes; "the police will keep it! Come to-morrow, with your keys, to Prince Dolgorouki's house in the Tverskoi Place, at ten o'clock." The box was sealed; the police master hauled it into his drojki; in half-an-hour the cavalcade was gone. Next day the Treasurer, with his clerk and manager, drove into Moscow with their keys, and on arriving in the Tverskoi Place were smitten pale with news that no search for ruble notes had been ordered by the Prince."

"Who, then, was that colonel of gendarmes?"

"A thief; the master of police a thief; the four gendarmes were thieves; the four eminent citizens thieves!"

"And what was done?"

"Prince Dolgorouki sent for Rebrof, Head of the Police (a very fine head), and told him what these thieves had done. "Superb!" laughed Rebrof, as he heard the tale; and when the Prince had come to an end of his details, he again cried out, in genuine admiration, "Ha! superb! One man, and only one in Moscow, has the brain for such a deed. The thief is Simonoff. Give me a little time, say nothing to the world, and Simonoff shall be yours." Rebrof kept his word; in three months Simonoff was tried, found guilty on the clearest proof, and sentenced to the mines for life. Rebrof traced him through the cabmen, followed him to his haunts, learned what he had done with the scrip and bonds, and then arrested him in a public bath. The money—two hundred thousand rubles—he had shared and spent. 'Siberia,' cried the brazen rogue, when the judge pronounced his doom; 'Siberia is a jolly place; I have plenty of money, and shall have a merry time.' Had there been no false reports about the Cemetery, a theft like Simonoff's could hardly have taken place."

CHAPTER XXXI.

Ragoski.

RAGOSKI, another Cemetery of the Old Believers, in the suburbs of Moscow, has a different story, and belongs to a second branch of the Popular Church. There is a party of Old Believers "with priests" and a party "without priests." Ragoski belongs to the party With Priests; Preobrajenski to the party Without Priests.

One party in the Popular Church believes that the Priesthood has been lost; the other party believes that it has been saved. Both parties deny the Orthodox Church; but the more liberal branch of the Popular Church allows that a true Priesthood may exist in other Greek communions, by the Bishops of which a line of genuine pastors may be ordained.

"You wish to visit the Ragoski?" asks my host. "Then we must look to our means. The chiefs of Ragoski are suspicious; and no wonder; the times of Persecution are near them still. In the reign of Nicolas, the Ragoski was shut up, the treasury was seized, and many of the worshippers were sent away —no one knows whither; to Siberia, to Archangel, to Imeritia—who shall say? Alexander has given them back their own; but they cannot tell how long the reign of grace may last. An order from Prince

Dolgorouki might come to-morrow; their property might be seized, their chapel closed, their hospital emptied, and their graves profaned. It is not likely; it is not probable; for the favour shown to this Cemetery is a part of our general progress, not an isolated act of imperial grace. But these Old Believers, caring little about general progress, give the glory to God. If you told them they are tolerated, as Jews are tolerated, they would think you mad; 'the Lord giveth, and the Lord taketh away; blessed be the name of the Lord.' Who among them knows when the evil day may come? Hence, they suspect a stranger. Not twenty men in Moscow, out of their own communion, have been within their gates. The Cemetery will be hard to enter; hard as to enter your own Abode of Love."

By happy chance, a gentleman calls while we are talking of ways and means, who is not only an Old Believer, but an Old Believer of the branch With Priests. A short man, white and wrinkled, with a keen grey eye, a serious face, and speech that takes you by its wonderful force and fire; this gentleman is a trader in the city, living in a fine house, and giving away in charities the income of a prince. I know one man to whom he sends every year a thousand rubles, as a help for poor students at the University. This good citizen is a banker, trader, mill-owner, what not; he is able, prompt, adroit; he gives good dinners; and is hand and glove with every one in power. I have heard folk say—by way of parable, no doubt—that all the police of Moscow are in his pay. You also hear whispers that this banker, trader, what not, is a priest; not of the ordained and apostolic order, but one of those popular priests, whom the Synod hunts to death. Who knows?

"You are an Old Believer," he begins, addressing his speech to me. "I know that from your book on The Holy Land; every word of which expresses the doctrines held by the Russian Church in her better days."

My host explains my great desire to see the Cemetery of Ragoski. "You shall be welcomed there like a friend. Let me see; shall I go with you? No; it will be better for you to go alone. The governor, Ivan Kruchinin, shall be there to receive you. I will write." He dashes off a dozen lines of introduction, written in the tone and haste of a recognised chief.

Armed with this letter we start next day, and driving through the court-yards of the Kremlin, have to pull up our drojki, to allow a train of big black horses to go prancing by. It is the train of Innocent, metropolite of Moscow, taking the air in a coach-and-six!

"This Ragoski Cemetery," says the Councillor of State, as we push through the China Town into the suburbs, "had an origin like that of the Transfiguration. It was opened on account of the plague (1770); not by a single founder, like its rival, but by a company of pious persons, anxious to consecrate the ground in which they had already begun to lay their dead. A chapel was erected, and a daily service was performed in that chapel for eighty-six years. Of late, the police are said to have troubled them very much; no one knows why; and no one dares to ask any questions on such a point. We are all too much afraid of the gentlemen in cowl and gown."

In about an hour we are at the gates. The place is like a desert, brightened by one gaudy pile. An open yard and silent office; a wall of brick; a painted chapel, in the old Russ style; a huge tabernacle of plain red brick; a wilderness of mounds and tombs:—this is Ragoski. Not a soul is seen, except one aged man in homely garb, who is carrying logs of wood. This man uncaps as we drive past; but turns and watches us with furtive eyes. Our letter is soon sent in; but we are evidently scanned like pilgrims at Marsaba; and twenty minutes elapse before the governor comes to us, cap in hand, and begs us to walk in.

A small, round man, with ruddy face and laughing eyes, and tender, plaintive manner, Ivan Kruchinin is not much like the men we see about —men who have a lean, sad look and fearful eyes, as though they lived in the conscious eclipse of light and faith. Coming to our carriage-door, he begs us to step in, and puts his service smilingly at our will.

"What is this new edifice with the gay old Tartar lozenges and bars?"

"Ugh!" sighs the governor.

"One of the last efforts made to win these Old Believers over," says the Councillor of State. "You see the monks have gone to work with craft. The pile is Russ outside, like many old chapels in Moscow; piles which catch the eye and impress the mind. They call it an Old Believers' Chapel; they have built it as the Roman centurion built the Jews a synagogue; and they hold a service in it, as they hold a service in the Transfiguration; said and sung by Orthodox popes, but in the language and the forms employed before Nikon's time."

Inside, the chapel is arranged to suit an Old Believer's taste; and every point of ritual, phrase, and form, is yielded to such as will accept the ministry of an Orthodox priest.

"Do they draw any part of your flock?"

"Not a soul," says the Governor. "A few of those 'without priests,' have joined them in despair; not many—not a hundred; while thousands of their people are coming round to us."

"These converts, who accept an Orthodox priest and the Ancient ritual, are called the United Old Believers—are they not?"

"United! They—the new schismatics! We know them not; we hate all sects; and these misguided men are adding to our country another sect."

Passing the cemetery yards, ascending some broad stone steps, we stand at a chapel door. This door is closed, and all around us reigns the silence which befits a tomb. Kruchinin makes a sign; his tap is answered from within; a door swings back; and out upon us floats a low, weird chant. Going through the door, we find ourselves in a spacious church, columned and pictured, with a noble dome.

This is the Old Believers' church. A few dim lamps are burning on the shrines; some tapers flit and mingle near the royal gates; a crowd of women kneel on the iron floor, not only in the aisles, but across the nave. Advancing, with our guide, up the central aisle, we come upon a line of men, some prostrate on the ground, some standing erect in prayer. A group of singers and readers stands apart, in front of the royal gates, with service-books and candles in their hands, reciting in a sweet, monotonous drone the ritual of the day.

As a surprise the scene is perfect.

"Who are these readers and singers?"

"Citizens of Moscow," says the governor; "bankers, farmers, men of every trade and class."

We stand aside until the service ends—a most impressive service, with louder prayers and livelier bendings than you hear and see in Orthodox cathedrals. Then we move about. "What is the service just concluded?" Kruchinin bends his eyes to the ground, and answers, "Only a laymen's service; one that can be said without a priest. You noticed, perhaps, that neither the royal gates nor the deacon's doors were opened?"

"Yes; how is that?"

"Our altars have been sealed."

"Your altars sealed!"

"Yes; you shall see. Come round this way;" and the governor leads us to the deacon's door. Sealed; certainly sealed; the door being nailed by a piece of leather to the screen; and the leather itself attached by a fresh blotch of official wax. It looks as if the Persecution were come again.

"How can such things be done?"

"Our Emperor does not know it," sighs the governor, who seems to be a thoroughly patriotic man; "it is the doing of our clerical police. We ask to have the use of our own altar, in our own church, according to the law. They say we shall have it, on one condition. They will give us our altar if we accept their priest!"

"And you refuse?"

"What can we do? Their priests have not been properly ordained; they have lost their virtue; they cannot give the blessing and absolve from sin. We have declined; our altars continue sealed; and our people have to sing and pray, as in the synagogues of Galilee, without a priest."

"That was not always so?"

"In other days we had our clergy, living with us openly in the light of day; but when our Cemetery was restored to us by our good Emperor in 1856, some trouble came upon us from the Synod on the subject of consecration, and we have not yet lived that trouble down."

"The prelates in St. Isaac's Square object to your priests receiving ordination at the hands of foreign bishops?"

"Yes; they wish us to receive the Holy Spirit from them; from men who have it not to give! We cannot live a lie; and we decline their offer to consecrate our priests."

"You have no popular priests?"

"No."

"If you have no priests, how can you marry and baptize infants?"

"According to the law of God."

"Without a priest?"

"No; with a priest. We have a priest for such things; though we cannot suffer him to risk Siberia by performing a public office in our church. Father Anton lives in secret. In the bazaar of Moscow, he is known as a merchant, dealing in grain and stuffs. The world knows nothing else about him; even the police have never suspected *him* of being a priest."

"He is ordained?"

"You know that some of our brethren live in Turkey and in Austria, where the Turks and Germans grant them asylums which they have not always found at home. A good many Old Believers dwell in a village called Belia Krinitza in the country lying at the feet of the Carpathians, just beyond the frontiers of Podolia and Bessarabia. One Ambrosius, a Greek prelate from Bulgaria, visited these refugees, and consecrated their Bishop Cyril, who is still alive. Cyril consecrated Father Anton, our Moscow priest."

"Father Anton marries and christens the members of your church?"

"He does, in secret. In his worldly name, he buys and sells, like any other dealer in his shop."

"You live in hope that the Persecution will not come again?"

"We live to suffer, and *not* to yield."

Passing into the hospital, we find a hundred men in one large edifice; four hundred women in a second large edifice. The rooms are very clean; the beds arranged in rows, the kitchens and baking houses bright. A woman stands at a desk before a Virgin, and reads out passages from the Gospels and the Psalms. Each poor old creature drops a curtsey as we pass her bed, and after we have eaten of their bread and salt, in the common dining-hall, they gather in a line and cross themselves, bending to the ground, thanking us, as though we had conferred on them some special grace.

These asylums of the Old Believers are the only free charities in Russia; for the hospitals in towns are government works, supported by the State. The Black Clergy does little for the poor, except supply them with crops of saints, and bring down Persecution on the Popular Church.

On driving back to Moscow, in the afternoon—pondering on what we have seen and heard—the lay singers, the clean asylum, and the sealed-up altar—we arrive under the Kremlin wall in time to find the mitred monk in our front again, just dashing with his splendid coach and six black horses through the Holy Gate!

CHAPTER XXXII.

Dissenting Politics.

THE revolution made by Nikon, ending in the rupture of his church, gave vast importance to dissenting bodies, while opening up a field for missionaries and impostors of every kind. Before his reign as Patriarch, the chief dissidents were the Eunuchs, the Self-burners, the Flagellants, the Sabbath-keepers, and the Silent Men; all of whom could trace their origin to foreign sources and distant times. They had no strong grip on the public mind. But, in setting up a state religion—an official religion—a persecuting religion—from which a majority of the people held aloof in scorn and fear, the Patriarch provided a common ground on which the wildest spirits could meet and mix. Aiming at one rule for all, the government put these Old Believers on a level with Flagellants and Eunuchs; the most conservative men in Russia with the most revolutionary men in Europe. All shades of difference were confounded by an ignorant police, inspired in their malign activities by a band of ignorant monks. So long as the Persecution lasted, a man who would not go to his parish church, pray in the new fashion, cross himself in the legal way, and bend his knee to Baal, was classed as a separatist and treated by the civil power as a man false to his Emperor and his God.

Thus the Old Believers came to support such bodies as the Milk Drinkers and Champions of the Holy Spirit, much as the old English Catholics joined hands with Quakers and Millennialists in their common war against a persecuting Church. These dissidents have learned to keep their own secrets, and to fight the persecutor with his own carnal weapons. They, too, keep spies. They have secret funds. They place their friends on the press. They send agents to court whom the Emperor never suspects. They have relations with monks and ministers, with bishops and aides-de-camp; they not unfrequently occupy the position of monk and minister, bishop and aide-de-camp. They go to church; they confess their sins; they help the parish priest in his need; they give money to adorn convents; and in some important cases they don the cowl and take religious vows. These persons are not easily detected in their guile; unless, indeed, fanaticism takes with them a visible shape. In passing through the province of Harkof, I hear in whispers of a frightful secret having come to light; no less than a discovery by the police that in the great monastery of Holy Mount, in that province, a number of Eunuchs are living in the guise of Orthodox monks!

Every day the Council is surprised by reports that some man noted for his piety and charity is a dissenter; nay, is a dissenting pope; though he owns a great mill and seems to devote his energies to trade.

The reigning Emperor, hating deceit, and most of all self-deceit, looks steadily at the facts. No doubt, if he could put these dissidents down, he would; but, like a man of genius, he knows that he must work in this field of thought by wit and not by power. "No illusions, gentlemen." From the first year of his reign he has been asking for true reports, and searching into the statements made with a steadfast yearning to find the truth.

What comes of his study, is now beginning to be seen of men. The Official Church has not ceased to be official, and even tyrannical; but the violence of her Persecution is going down; the regular clergy have been softened; the monkish fury has been curbed; and lay opinion has been coaxed into making a first display of strength.

A Minute was laid by the Emperor before his Council of Ministers so early as Oct. 15 and 27, 1858, for their future guidance in dealing with dissenters; under which title the Holy Governing Synod still classed the Old Believers with the Flagellants and Eunuchs! The Minute written by his father was not removed from the books; it was simply explained and carried forward; yet the change was radical; since the police, in all their dealings with religious bodies, were instructed to talk in a gentler tone, and to give accused persons the benefit of every doubt which should occur on points of law. A change of spirit is often of higher moment than a change of phrase. Without implying that either his father was wrong, or the Holy Governing Synod unjust, the Emperor opened a door by which many of the nonconformists could at once escape. But what was done only shows too plainly how much remains to do. The Emperor has checked the persecutor's arm; he has not crushed the persecuting spirit.

A Special Committee was named by him to study the whole subject of dissent; with the practical view of seeing how far it could be conscientiously tolerated, and in what way it could be honestly repressed.

This Committee made their report in August 1864; a voluminous document (of which some folios only have been printed); and adopting their report, the Emperor added to the paper a second Minute, which is still the rule of his ministers in dealing with such affairs. In this Minute he recognises the existence of dissent. He acknowledges that dissidents may have civil and religious rights. Of course, as head of the Church, he cannot suffer that Church to be injured; but he desires his ministers, after taking counsel with the Holy Governing Synod, and obtaining their consent at every step, to see that justice is always done.

The spirit of this Imperial Minute is so good that the monks attack it; not in open day and with honest words; for such is not their method and their manner; but with sly suggestions in the confessor's closet and serpentine whispers near the sacred shrines. It is unpopular with the Holy Governing Synod. But the conservatives and sectaries, long cast down, look up into what they call a new heaven and a new earth. They say the day of peace has come, and finding a door of appeal thrown open to them in St. Petersburg, they are sending in hundreds of petitions; here requesting leave to open a cemetery, there to construct an altar, here again to build a church. In thirty-two months (Jan. 1866 to Sept. 1868), the Home Ministry received no less than 367 petitions of various kind.

Valouef, the Minister in power when this Imperial Minute was first drawn up, had a difficult part to play between his liberal master and the retrograde monks. No man is strong enough to quarrel with the tribunal sitting in St. Isaac's Square; and Valouef was wrecked by his zeal in carrying out the imperial plan. The Minister had to get these Fathers to consent in every case to the petitioner's prayer; these Fathers who thought dissenters had no right to live, and kept on quoting to him the edicts of Nicolas, as though that sovereign were still alive! On counting his papers at the end of those thirty-two months of trial, Valouef found that out of 367 petitions in his office, the Holy Governing Synod consented to his granting twenty-one, postponing fifty, and rejecting all the rest.

A man, who said he was born in the official Church, begged leave to profess dissenting doctrine, which he had come to see was right:—refused. A merchant offered to build a chapel for dissenters in a dissenting village:—refused. A builder proposed to throw a wall across a convent garden, so as to divide the male from the female part:—refused. A dissenting minister asked to be relieved from the daily superintendence of his city police:—refused. Michaeloff, a rich merchant of St. Petersburg, offered to found a hospital for the use of dissenters near the capital, at his personal charge:—refused. Last year an asylum for poor dissenters was opened at Kaluga; an asylum built by peasants for persons of their class:—the Synod orders it to be closed.

Hundreds of petitions come in from Archangel, Siberia, and the Caucasus, from men who were in other days transported to those districts for conscience sake, requesting leave to come back. These petitions are divided by the Holy Governing Synod into two groups: (1) those of men who have been judged by some kind of court; (2) those of men who have been exiled by a simple order of the police. The first class are refused in mass without inquiry; a few of the second class, after counsel taken with the provincial quorum, are allowed.

From these examples, it will be seen that the liberal movement is not reckless; but the movement is along the line; the work goes on; and every day some progress is being made. A minister who has to work with a board of monks must feel his way.

CHAPTER XXXIII.

Conciliation.

ONE point has been gained in the mere fact of the Imperial Minute having drawn a distinction between things which may be thought and things which may be done. The right of holding a particular article of faith, stands on a different ground to the right of preaching that article of faith in open day. The first is private, and concerns oneself; the second is public, and concerns the general weal. What is private only may be left to conscience; what is public must be always subject to the law.

The ministers have come to see that every man has a right to think for himself about his duty to God; and under their directions the police have orders to leave a man alone, so long as he refrains from exciting the public mind, and disturbing the public peace. In fact, the Russians have been brought into line with their neighbours the Turks.

In Moscow, a man is now as free to believe what he likes, as he would be in Stamboul; though he must exercise his liberty in both these cities with the deference due from the unit to the mass. He must not meddle with the dominant creed. He must not trifle with the followers of that creed; though his action on other points may be perfectly free. Having full possession of the field, the Church will not allow herself to be attacked; even though it should please her to fall on you with fire and sword.

In Moscow, a Mussulman may try to convert a Jew; in Stamboul, an Armenian may try to convert a Copt; but woe to the Mussulman in Russia who tempts a Christian to his mosque, to the Christian in Turkey who tempts a Mussulman to his church! As on the higher, so it stands on the lower plane. The right of propagand lies with the ruling power. In Russia, a monk may try to convert a dissenter; the dissenter will be sent to Siberia should he happen to convert the monk. A rule exactly parallel holds in Turkey and in Persia, where a mollah may try to convert a giaour; but the giaour will be beaten and imprisoned should he have the misfortune to convert the mollah.

Some men may fancy that little has been gained so long as toleration stops at free thought, and interdicts free speech. In England or America that would seem true and even trite; but the rules applied to Moscow are not the rules which would be suitable in London or New York. The gain is vast, when a man is permitted to say his prayers in peace.

One day last week I came upon striking evidence of the value of this freedom. Riding into a large village, known to me by fame for its dissenting virtues, I exclaimed, on seeing the usual Orthodox domes and crosses, "Not many dissidents here!" My companion smiled. A moment later we entered the elder's house. "Have you any Old Believers here?"

"Yes, many."

"But here is a church, big enough to hold every man, woman, and child in your village."

"Yes, that is true. You find it empty now; in other times you might have found it full."

"How was that? Were your people drawn away from their Ancient rites?"

"Never. We were driven to church by the police. When God gave us Alexander, we left off going to mass."

"Was the Persecution sharp?"

"So sharp, that only four stout men lived through it; never going to church for a dozen years. When Nicolas died, the police pretended that we had only those four Old Believers in this place; the next day it was suspected, the next year it was known, that every soul in it was an Old Believer."

All these dissenting bodies are political parties, more or less openly pronounced; and have to be dealt with on political, no less than on religious grounds. Rejecting the State Church, they reject the Emperor, so far as he assumes to be head of that Church. A state Church, they say, is Antichrist; a devil's kingdom, set up by Satan himself in the form of Nikon the Monk. So far as Alexander is a royal prince, they take him, and even pray for him; but they will not place his image in their chapel; they refuse to pray for him as a true believer; and they fear he is dead to religion, and lost to God.

The Popular Church contends that since the reign of Peter the Great everything has been lawless and provisional. Peter, they say, was a bastard son of Nikon the Monk; in other words, of the devil himself. The first object of this child of the Evil One being to destroy the Russian people, he abandoned the country, and built him a palace among the Swedes and Finns. His second object being to destroy the Russian church, he abolished the office of Patriarch, and made himself her spiritual chief.

The consequences which they draw from these facts are instant and terrible; for these consequences touch with a deadly sorcery the business of their daily lives.

Since Satan began his reign in the person of Peter the Great, all authorities and rules have been suspended on the earth. According to them, nothing is lawful, for the reign of law is over. Contracts are waste; no trust can be executed; no sacrament can be truly held; not even that of marriage. Hence, it is a matter of conscience with thousands of Old Believers, that they shall not undergo the nuptial rite. They live without it, in the hope of Heaven providing them with a remedy on earth for what would otherwise be a wrong in heaven. And thus their lives are passed in the shadow of a terrible doom.

The absence of marriage-ties among the best of these Old Believers is not the least frightful evil. So far as the men and women are concerned, the case is bad enough; but as regards their children, it is worse. These children are regarded by the law as basely born. "By the devil's law," say the Old Believers sadly; but the fact remains, that under the Russian code these "bastards" do not inherit their fathers' wealth. In other states, an issue might be found in the making of a will, by which a father could dispose of his property to his children as he pleased. But an Old Believer dares not make a will. A will is a public act, and he disclaims the present public powers. The common course is, for an Old Believer to *give* his money to some friend whom he can trust, and for that friend to *give it back* to his children when he is no more.

The Emperor, studying remedies for these grave disorders among his people, has conceived the bold idea of legalising in Russia the system of civil marriage, already established in every free country of Europe, and in each of the United States. A bill has been drawn, so as to spare the Orthodox clergy as much as could be done. The Council of State is favourable to this bill; but the Holy Governing Synod, frightened at all these changes, refuse to admit that a "sacrament" can be given by a magistrate; and a bill which would bring peace and order into a million of households is delayed, though it is not likely to be sacrificed, in deference to their monastic doubts.

"What else would you have the Emperor do?" I ask a man of confidence in this Popular Church.

"Do! Restore our ancient rights. In Nikon's time, the Crown procured our condemnation by a Council of the Eastern churches; we survive the curse; and now we ask to have that ban removed."

"You stand condemned by a Council?"

"Yes; by a deceived and corrupted Council. That curse must be taken off our heads."

"Is the government aware of your demands?"

"It is aware."

"Have any steps been taken to that end?"

"A great one. Alexander has proposed to remove the ban; and even the Synod, calling itself holy, has consented to recall the curse; but we reject all offers from this band of monks; they have no power to bind and loose. The Eastern churches put us in the wrong; the Eastern churches must concur to set us right. They cursed us in their ignorance; they must bless us in their knowledge. We have passed through fire, and know our weakness and our strength. No other method will suffice. We ask a general Council of the Oriental church."

"Can the Emperor call that Council?"

"Yes; if Russia needs it for her peace; and who can say she does not need it for her peace?"

END OF VOL. I.

www.ingramcontent.com/pod-product-compliance
Lightning Source LLC
Chambersburg PA
CBHW052213240426
43670CB00037B/433